AN INVITATION
TO LOVE

Other Loyola Press books by William A. Barry

Changed Heart, Changed World

A Friendship Like No Other

Here's My Heart, Here's My Hand

Letting God Come Close

Praying the Truth

Seek My Face

AN INVITATION TO LOVE

A Personal Retreat on the Great Commandment

WILLIAM A. BARRY, SJ

LOYOLAPRESS.
A JESUIT MINISTRY

Chicago

LOYOLA PRESS.
A JESUIT MINISTRY

3441 N. Ashland Avenue
Chicago, Illinois 60657
(800) 621-1008
www.loyolapress.com

Imprimi Potest: Very Rev. John J. Cecero, SJ

Scripture quotations contained herein are from the *New Revised Standard Version Bible: Catholic Edition*, copyright © 1993 and 1989 by the Division of Christian Education of the National Council of the Churches of Christ in the U.S.A. Used by permission. All rights reserved.

Nick Genovese's article, "My Family Disagrees about Donald Trump—But That Won't Divide Us," was first published in *America*, December 7, 2016, www.americamagazine.org/politics-society/2016/12/07/ and is used by permission.

James Martin's article, "A Week in Rome with Jesuits, and I Saw God at Work Far beyond the Vatican," *America*, January 2, 2017, www.americamagazine.org/faith/2016/12/16/james-martin-week-rome-jesuits-and-i-saw-god-work-far-beyond-vatican is used by permission.

All quotations from Ignatius of Loyola, including those from his Spiritual Exercises, are from Ignatius of Loyola, *Personal Writings*, trans. Joseph A. Munitiz and Philip Endean (London: Penguin Books, 1996).

Cover art credit: IakovKalinin/iStock/Getty Images

ISBN: 978-0-8294-4667-8
Library of Congress Control Number: 2018947532

Printed in the United States of America.
18 19 20 21 22 23 24 25 26 27 Versa 10 9 8 7 6 5 4 3 2 1

For William C. Russell, SJ, and Darrell A. Jones

Teach me to seek you,
and reveal yourself to me as I seek:
For unless you instruct me
I cannot seek you,
and unless you reveal yourself
I cannot find you.
Let me seek you in desiring you:
let me desire you in seeking you.
Let me find you in loving you:
let me love you in finding you.

—St. Anselm of Canterbury

Contents

Preface

About six years ago, I finished writing *Praying the Truth* and for a long time thought that I had come to the end of my writing days. I did not have any ideas for new writing or even a desire to write. A few years ago, I thought of writing a book on the two great commandments, love of God and love of neighbor, and even started a file for it on my computer. But I never got to the point of beginning to write until the summer of 2016, when, during my annual retreat, I decided to fish or cut bait, as it were—to begin writing to see if I had anything to say that might be helpful to others. To my surprise and joy, things started to come rather easily, and I was able to do the book you now have in your hands.

As you will see, almost from the first page, this is not a book about the meaning of the two commandments—which, for the purposes of this book, are considered the one great commandment—and still less an exhortation to the reader to fulfill them. Rather, it's an invitation to anyone who wants to grow in love for God and neighbor, an invitation to try some prayerful exercises that I and others have found helpful. I hope you will, as well.

PART 1

LOVE IS THE FOUNDATION

The United States and many other countries are currently roiled by seemingly unresolvable political, racial, economic, and ecological conflicts. Given these circumstances, you may wonder why I'm writing a book on the two great commandments: love of God and love of neighbor. It may seem that, like the emperor Nero, I'm fiddling while our country burns to the ground. Yet I can think of nothing more important for us human beings to do in such perilous times than to love God and our neighbors. Let me explain and, in the process, give readers an idea of what they are getting into by picking up this book.

The Bible, the whole of it, is not about how to get to heaven when we die. It's about God's dream for his good creation. God creates a world for a purpose and human beings to be God's images in this world and thus cooperate with God in that purpose or dream. Many Jews of Jesus' time, and Jesus himself, summed up what it means to be a human being with the two great commandments: to love God and to love our neighbor as ourselves. The Bible is the story of God's efforts to get us to live as human beings—that is, as images of God. This book is designed to help people live God's dream and thus become part of the solution to our world's seemingly insoluble difficulties rather than part of the problem.

Imagine a world in which everyone loved God and neighbor. It would be a world without hunger, without crime, without any fear, wouldn't it? In such a world, everyone would be cared for, so no one would need to expend undue energy or anxiety on his or her own needs. This is God's dream for our world, as we shall see. But it will come about only if individuals—and, through them, communities—really do love one another in an effective way. Thus, my passion for writing this retreat. We really are invited by God to help God transform this world, to help God bring about what Jesus called the kingdom of God.

All of us have heard these two commandments often. But if you're like me, you have trouble living up to their demands. Over the years I have found different ways to help myself and others move closer to being able to love God and neighbor.

I would like to offer some of the ways people have found helpful in growing in their love for God and in their love for neighbor.

I intend this book not to be a theoretical study of the two commandments, still less as an effort to convince you of their merit. Rather, I presume that you already know the commandments but may find fulfilling them difficult or, in some cases, impossible. However, you want to love God and neighbor better and so may be interested in trying out ways to grow in these loves and thus become more a part of God's solution for our world.

How to Use This Book

Each **prayer session** will present material from the Bible, from literature, from hymns, and from life that might help you tap into this desire that God has planted in your heart. You may not be moved by some of the suggestions. Not to worry; that's true of everyone. Use only what you find helpful. I've provided many different suggestions, and each session has a different theme. I also suggest when you might take a rest from prayer for a time. I include these suggestions not as a demand to stop but as a reminder that few of us can pray for hours on end and that you need to move through the book at a leisurely pace.

If you want to grow in your love for God and your neighbor, I suggest that there is no better way than to take on a regular practice of prayer and reflection, and this requires some discipline and a devotion to practices—another reason for you to move through this material at a realistic pace. Better to pray a little and slowly with regularity than try to pray a lot in a rush but with little engagement and then lose interest.

You will also notice that I make suggestions for beginning each reading period or prayer period. I will often refer to these suggestions as a reminder. They have been found to help people engage more personally and prayerfully with the material that follows.

Which Commandment Is the First of All?

In all three of the Gospels that are related to one another—Matthew, Mark, and Luke—Jesus is asked, "Which commandment is the first of all?" (Mark 12:28; Matthew 22:34–40; Luke 10:25–29). In Mark, the questioner is friendly; in Matthew and Luke, unfriendly. In Mark and Matthew, Jesus himself gives the answer; in Luke, Jesus turns the question on the questioner. In all three Gospels, the answer is fundamentally the same—here from Mark: "The first is, 'Hear, O Israel: The Lord our God, the Lord is one; you shall love the Lord your God with all your heart, and with all your soul, and with all your mind, and with all your strength.' The second is this, 'You shall love your neighbor as yourself.' There is no other commandment greater than these" (Mark 12:29–31). In this passage, the questioner commends Jesus for this answer, and Jesus, in turn, tells him, "You are not far from the kingdom of God" (32–33).

In the first part of his answer, Jesus recites what every believing Jew says at least twice a day. These words are called the *Shema Ysrael*, "Hear, O Israel," because they are the first words of the commandment in Hebrew, as found in Deuteronomy 6:4–5. "Hear, O Israel: The LORD is our God, the LORD alone. You shall love the LORD your God with all your heart, and with all your soul, and with all your might." The second commandment comes from Leviticus 19:18: "You shall not take vengeance or bear a grudge against any of your people, but you shall love your neighbor as yourself: I am the LORD." Clearly, for Jesus and for his interlocutors, both friendly and unfriendly, these two commandments contain the essence of the Mosaic law. Indeed, in Mark, Jesus' response to the questioner at the end of the passage indicates that living out these two commandments is what the kingdom of God is all about.

Notice that last line: "living out these two commandments is what the kingdom of God is all about." The Gospels make it clear: Jesus believed that with his life and ministry, God was taking the decisive final step in the great design God had in creating this universe. Jesus spoke of this final step as leading to the "kingdom of God," his shorthand for what he was about in his life and ministry and what he was calling all his followers to cooperate in building up. The kingdom of God is not about getting as many of us as possible into heaven after we die; it's what God wants in creating this universe. In a later session you will reflect prayerfully on God's great risk in creating the world with us human beings as God's images and likenesses. God invites us to join in the great adventure begun with creation, to cooperate with God in bringing about the kingdom of God in which human beings live in harmony with God, with one another, and with the whole created world. The kingdom of God is not about some heavenly realm outside this world; it's about this world in which we live. How we live here and now has enormous consequences for all of creation and for God.

The Bible as a Five-Act Play

The whole of the Bible, from the book of Genesis to the book of Revelation, reveals God's creative and providential work of bringing about in history what God intends with creation. In *Jesus and the Victory of God*, N. T. Wright, the Anglican bishop and biblical scholar, likens the whole of the Bible to a five-act Shakespearean play but one in which the last act is left up to the actors themselves, with their knowledge of the story of the first four acts.

- The **first act** of God's story includes the two stories of creation in Genesis chapters 1—2. God creates a good creation with human beings as God's images, called to cooperate with God in developing creation.

- The **second act** begins with human folly, the decision of the first humans not to trust God but to trust in themselves and in the serpent, which symbolizes Satan. Chapter 3 of Genesis begins this second act. That folly leads to the loss of innocence, the growth of fear and hiding from God, the killing of Abel by his brother Cain, other murders, rape, incest, death at an earlier and earlier age, the destructive Flood in Noah's time, and finally, in chapter 11, the building of the tower of Babel and the inability of humans to understand one another.

- But all is not lost, because chapter 12 of Genesis ushers in the **third act:** the call of Abraham and Sarah with God's promise that, because of their faith in God, they will be the origin of the chosen people, the Israelites. This third act covers the rest of what we Christians call the Old Testament, a long story of this chosen people's fidelity and infidelity to the covenant God had made with them in the desert.

- From this people comes Jesus of Nazareth, whose life, death, and resurrection are the **fourth act.**
- The **fifth act** begins with Pentecost, when the Spirit of God descends on the disciples of Jesus, and is ongoing. We Christians are asked to carry on the work of Jesus with the help of the Spirit. This retreat is about how to carry on that great work.

To Bear the Beams of Love

The English poet and visionary William Blake once wrote, "We are put on earth for a little space, that we may learn to bear the beams of love" (79). Blake assumes that it's hard for us to bear the beams of love. Many, if not most, of us seem to want love, from God or from others, but only in small doses. I have to say that I shy away from the direct expressions of love from others. Even God has a tough time convincing me of his love. I seem psychologically geared to believe that I need to earn the love of others, even God. So I must learn to bear the beams of love, especially when I realize that there is no way that I can or need to *earn* God's love. God's love for us has nothing to do with our deserving it; it just is the way God is.

Neither do I find it easy to love God with my whole heart, soul, mind, and strength or to love my neighbor as myself.

It's easy enough to say the words, except that honesty requires me to confess that my heart, soul, mind, and strength are not really in line with what I say. There are moments when my heart is fully intent on God, and I mean these words. But most of the time, my heart and mind are otherwise engaged; God seems far from my interest. Flannery O'Connor speaks for me and for many others, and perhaps for you, when she writes in her journal, "Dear God, I cannot love Thee the way I want to. . . . I do not know you God because I am in the way. Please help me to push myself aside" (*The New Yorker*, "My Dear God: A Young Writer's Prayers," September 16, 2013, 26).

Pause for a few moments and consider these questions.

- What is your gut response to the commandment to love God with your whole heart, soul, mind, and strength: hope? Guilt? Skepticism? Whatever your reaction, tell it to God. Start from your most honest place.
- Are you able to pray a prayer similar to Flannery O'Connor's? If you can, pray these words or something like them: Dear God, I cannot love Thee the way I want to. I do not know you, God, because I am in the way. Please help me to push myself aside.

We can come to love God because of all the gifts God gives us. We will spend some time on this motivation, especially through the eyes of Ignatius of Loyola's "Contemplation for Attaining Love for God" in his *Spiritual Exercises*.

But when all is said and done, to love God because of what God gives us may not get to the heart of what the first commandment intends. There are instances when love shows itself as true even when we get nothing from loving the other. Think of the wife who continues to visit and to care for her husband when he has Alzheimer's and no longer even recognizes her. We shall look at some instances of such love of others and of God.

Then there is this statement from the first letter of John: "Those who say, 'I love God,' and hate their brothers and sisters, are liars; for those who do not love a brother or sister whom they have seen, cannot love God whom they have not seen" (1 John 4:20). That's frightening, isn't it?

Can Love Be a Command?

Before we go on, let's get one issue out of the way. Do you find it a bit odd to be *commanded* to love God—or anyone else, for that matter? I do. Commanded love seems a contradiction in terms. It might be motivated more by fear than by anything else. The first letter of John says, "There is no fear in love, but perfect love casts out fear; for fear has to do with punishment, and whoever fears has not reached perfection in love" (1 John 4:18). Love, even of God, can only be given freely. Love under threat, which a command seems to entail, would almost always be suspect: "Does he really mean it, or is he just saying that he loves me because he's afraid of me?" You might object, "But wouldn't God know the difference between feigned love and the real article?" However, we are not God, and we would never be sure that we really loved God or anyone else, nor would we ever be sure of anyone else's love of us if love could be coerced. At any rate, I'm not satisfied with any argument I've heard that love can be commanded.

This leaves us with a dilemma. There is no question that most translations of Deuteronomy and Leviticus use the word *commandment*, as do most translations of the New Testament, which have Jesus quoting Deuteronomy and Leviticus. What are we to make of this? It might help to know that the Hebrew word translated "command" can be understood as "teaching," a less coercive way of understanding what is being proposed. In other words, Deuteronomy and Leviticus and the New Testament are instructing us how to live as images of God in this world.

Maybe we can look at all the commandments in this way. You may remember them from your early religious learning. I cite them as I remember them: "You shall not take the name of the Lord your God in vain; remember to keep holy the Lord's Day; honor your father and your mother; you shall not kill; you shall not commit adultery; you shall not steal; you shall not bear false witness against your neighbor; you shall not covet your neighbor's wife; you shall not covet your neighbor's goods." My own best thought is that God lays these out before his people as the best way to be human beings. Remember that Genesis tells us that God created us in his image and likeness. God is telling the Israelites and us that obedience to these "teachings" is the best way to be human and, thus, ultimately happy.

Suggestions for Beginning Each Period of Prayer

First, you might start with the prayer of St. Anselm that appears in the frontispiece of the book. Anselm wrote that prayer in the eleventh century just before he began to write his proof for the existence of God. In other words, he wanted God to be with him as he wrote the paragraphs and chapters that followed. He wanted his rather abstract proof for God's existence to be written with God's gracious help. I prayed his prayer every time I began to write these prayer sessions. By doing so, I felt myself to be in God's presence. As you begin to read each prayer session, and, perhaps, before you engage in any of the prayer exercises I suggest, you might want to get into that same frame of mind by praying his prayer.

Second, recall that God is looking at you, waiting for you to be aware of his presence.

Third, ask God for what you want from this time of prayerful reading or contemplation. For instance, you might ask God to help you grow in your desire and ability to love God with all your heart, with all your soul, with all your mind, and with all your strength, and to love your neighbor as yourself. Another possibility is to use the following prayer from the Liturgy of the Hours: "Lord, our help and our guide, make your love the foundation of our lives. May our love for you express itself in our eagerness to do good for others. Grant this through our Lord Jesus Christ, your Son, who lives and reigns with you and the Holy Spirit, one God, for ever and ever. Amen" (1975 ed., 28th Sunday in Ordinary Time).

As a reminder in the rest of the book, I'll refer to these suggestions with these or similar words: "Remember the suggestions for beginning your prayer."

Also, note your reactions to the Scripture texts or literature cited. It may help to keep a journal as you go through these sessions. In it you can record your reactions and perhaps some words or thoughts that touched you most. You don't have to write for anyone but yourself; you can use abbreviations and words and phrases instead of whole sentences. My reason for this suggestion and the kinds of question I suggest throughout this book is twofold: First, your reactions will give you something to talk over with God in prayer. Second, these reactions will serve as valuable clues as you discern what is happening in your life. The section titled "On Discernment" at the end of the book provides some simple rules for discernment. You may find these helpful.

Throughout the book I will also suggest times to take a break, as a reminder that you need to take time between periods of reading and praying to do other things and also to let the insights and prayer have a chance to settle more deeply into your whole being. Now, let's begin.

> Teach me to seek you,
> and reveal yourself to me as I seek:
> For unless you instruct me
> I cannot seek you,
> and unless you reveal yourself
> I cannot find you.
> Let me seek you in desiring you:
> let me desire you in seeking you.

> Let me find you in loving you:
> let me love you in finding you.
>
> —St. Anselm of Canterbury

Sit quietly and consider this: God is looking at you with divine love and waits for you to be aware of God's presence.

Read the following Scripture verse two or three times and note your reaction to it:

> So God created humankind in his image,
>   in the image of God he created them;
> male and female he created them.
>
> —Genesis 1:27

Talk with God—or write in your journal—about how these words affect your thoughts and emotions.

Love Isn't Easy

As we begin this session, let's recall the suggestions for beginning every session of prayer and reading.

Very little in our culture makes it easy to love God and our neighbor. Too soon in childhood we learn to fear God and others. Fear gets in the way of love. Too soon also we learn to want things only because others have them; thus we are taught to be competitive with others. Fear, envy, and the desire to win out over others get in the way of loving others. Moreover, God can seem too distant and mysterious to be the sustained object of our love, and our love of neighbor may be limited to close family and friends. Many of us may well find these two great commandments beyond our powers to follow.

The apostle Paul addresses his own dismay and disgust with himself in the seventh chapter of his letter to the Romans.

> I find it to be a law that when I want to do what is good, evil lies close at hand. For I delight in the law of God in my inmost self, but I see in my members another law at war with the law of my mind, making me captive to the law of sin that dwells in my members. Wretched man that I am! Who will rescue me from this body of death? Thanks be to God through Jesus Christ our Lord!

Do these words, at times, ring true for you? You want to do something that you know is the right thing to do and, perhaps, the best thing for yourself, but you don't seem able to do it. I want to give up cigarettes, but I can't. I want to love God above all things, but I don't seem able to. People find this true about many things. For a moment, recall which sins you must confess repeatedly. Where does this conflict between desire and follow-through touch you most?

Addicts begin to turn the corner when they can admit the truth—namely, that they are helpless over their addiction. This is the first of the Twelve Steps of Alcoholics Anonymous. Like Paul, we can come close to despair of ever moving beyond this helplessness: "Wretched man that I am! Who will rescue me from this body of death?" (Romans 7:24) For his near-despair, Paul found the answer in Jesus. Faith in Jesus rescued him from his inability to do what he wanted to do. He spills a lot of ink in the letters to the Romans and to the Galatians trying to convince readers that it is only by the grace of God in Christ Jesus and faith in that grace that they are saved, not by their own efforts. I have become convinced from personal experience and from the experience of many others that we still need to hear this Pauline message repeatedly. In spite of evidence to the contrary, it is very hard for us to admit that we are not in control, at least of ourselves.

The disciples of Jesus experienced this inability to do what they wanted to do and what they had been able to do in other instances. Mark gives one example in chapter 9 of that Gospel. When Jesus came down from the mountain of the transfiguration with Peter, James, and John, he found that a man had brought his demon-possessed son to the other disciples, who could not cure him. When the son was brought to Jesus, the spirit convulsed the boy and threw him into a fit.

> Jesus asked the father, "How long has this been happening to him?" And he said, "From childhood. It has often cast him into the fire and into the water to destroy him; but if you are able to do anything, have pity on us and help us." Jesus said to him, "If you are able!—All things can be done for the one who believes." Immediately the father of

the child cried out, "I believe; help my unbelief!" (Mark 9:21–24)

When Jesus heard this wonderful prayer, he cast out the demon and restored the boy to his father. Later the disciples asked Jesus why they could not cast out the demon, and he replied, "This kind can come out only through prayer." Only God can cast him out. The father's prayer is one I say constantly because I know that my faith is shallow and needs deepening. Only God can help me; I cannot do it myself.

God can do what seems impossible. But we must believe this. Addicts who can say and mean the First Step—that their lives have become unmanageable and that they are powerless to change things—then face whether there is any hope for them. The Second Step expresses a hope; they have come to believe that there is "someone" who can help: God, a Higher Power. The Third Step asks them to put their unmanageable lives in the hands of God or of their Higher Power—to trust that God can do what seems impossible to them. This step is an act of faith. Alcoholics must trust that God will keep them alive without the drink that they feel they cannot live without. They discover that what Jesus says on another occasion in Mark's Gospel is true: "For mortals it [being saved] is impossible, but not for God; for God all things are possible" (Mark 10:27). Note that Jesus does not say that for mortals it is very hard; no, it's impossible. That's what alcoholics have found out through hard experience; they cannot stop drinking alcohol. When they can take this Third Step, they are on the road to recovery from their addiction.

It is difficult, even impossible, to love God with all your heart, soul, mind, and strength and your neighbor as yourself without God's help. But we must remember that "for God all things are possible." Perhaps we could recast the father's prayer for our purposes now: "I do love You and my neighbor, at least a little; help my lack of love." You may want to say this prayer or something like it often as you go through this retreat.

Pause for a few moments, and if it's in line with your true thoughts and feelings, pray,

"I do love You and my neighbor, at least a little; help my lack of love."

The Real World

The real world, for believers, is this one world in which we live, created by God to be a world in which human beings cooperate with God in making it a place where all live harmoniously with God, with one another, and with the rest of creation. The two "great commandments" are God's teaching on how to live in this world in such a way as to be part of God's solution for our world's problems rather than become part of the problem. In working your way through this retreat, you can learn to assist God in the great work of bringing about the kingdom of God.

In his book on resurrection and eternal life, *Is This All There Is?* Gerhard Lohfink makes a point that certainly rings true as we work through these prayer sessions: "[I]t is precisely when Christians are at home in the world, tasting its joys in gratitude, caring for it as a creation entrusted to us and giving ourselves to it in order to gain it for the reign of God—only then are we loving God" (255).

- Here is most of the long, traditional prayer attributed to St. Patrick. Read it through twice or more.
- Pay attention to the phrases or lines that draw your attention, that really speak what is in your own heart and mind today.
- Pray those phrases and lines or begin with them and create your own prayer.

> I arise today
> Through a mighty strength, the invocation of the Trinity,
> Through belief in the Threeness,

Through confession of the Oneness
of the Creator of creation.

I arise today
Through the strength of Christ's birth with His
baptism,
Through the strength of His crucifixion with His
burial,
Through the strength of His resurrection with His
ascension,
Through the strength of His descent for the
judgment of doom.

I arise today
Through the strength of the love of cherubim,
In the obedience of angels,
In the service of archangels,
In the hope of resurrection to meet with reward,
In the prayers of patriarchs,
In the predictions of prophets,
In the preaching of apostles,
In the faith of confessors,
In the innocence of holy virgins,
In the deeds of righteous [people].

I arise today, through
The strength of heaven,
The light of the sun,

The radiance of the moon,
The splendor of fire,
The speed of lightning,
The swiftness of wind,
The depth of the sea,
The stability of the earth,
The firmness of rock.

I arise today, through
God's strength to pilot me,
God's might to uphold me,
God's wisdom to guide me,
God's eye to look before me,
God's ear to hear me,
God's word to speak for me,
God's hand to guard me,
God's shield to protect me,
God's host to save me
From snares of devils,
From temptation of vices,
From everyone who shall wish me ill,
afar and near. . . .

Christ with me,
Christ before me,
Christ behind me,
Christ in me,
Christ beneath me,

Christ above me,
Christ on my right,
Christ on my left,
Christ when I lie down,
Christ when I sit down,
Christ when I arise,
Christ in the heart of every [person] who thinks
of me,
Christ in the mouth of everyone who speaks of me,
Christ in every eye that sees me,
Christ in every ear that hears me.

I arise today
Through a mighty strength, the invocation of the
Trinity,
Through belief in the Threeness,
Through confession of the Oneness
of the Creator of creation.

The Creation Story, Part 1: Acts of Mystery and Love

When I look at your heavens, the work of your fingers,
the moon and the stars that you have established;
what are human beings that you are mindful of them,
mortals that you care for them?

—Psalm 8:3–4

The psalmist looks at what God has created and, in that very act of looking at nature, finds himself loving and praising God. One time-honored prayer is simply to ponder what God has done in creation.

Try to imagine the Mystery we call God *without* this universe. It's almost impossible, isn't it? Yet we believe that God did not have to create anything. God was not lonely. But a universe that is not God and still is totally dependent on God does exist, and we know that it is vast and very, very old—at least 15 billion years old. Our planet and our existence on this planet are the products of eons and eons of evolution, such that the time of human existence is minute compared to the age of the whole universe. Try to get your mind and heart around the astronomical numbers involved here, and then let the quiet mystery hit you "that there is anything, anything at all, let alone cosmos, joy, memory, everything, rather than void," to quote poet Denise Levertov's "Primary Wonder."

> Pause for a few moments and ask God, "Why do you do it? Why do you lavish your love on us through your creation? Why even pay attention to us?" After you ask the question, try to be quiet for a few moments, at least, to give God a chance to respond.

One way to get a sense of God's immense creativity is to read prayerfully the first chapter of Genesis, letting the words touch your mind, heart, and imagination. This is the first story of creation, based on a tradition different from the story of creation that begins with Genesis 2:4, the story of the Garden of Eden and the first two humans. The story in the first chapter of Genesis envisages the creation of our world as occurring over six days, after which God rests on the seventh day. As you probably know, these traditions are not to be taken literally. They are written not to teach us about historical events but to draw us into the ongoing story of God's creative relationship with us humans.

So, if you wish, open your Bible—or go to a free online version of the Bible such as www.biblegateway.com or www.Bible.oremus.org. Prepare yourself for a prayerful reading. For now, limit yourself to the first 25 verses of Genesis, the story of the creation of everything except humans.

- How did the reading go for you?
- What, if anything, surprised you?
- Did you want to ask God anything as you were reading? Did you ask God? If not, why not ask now?
- Did you have a sense of God being with you? If so, how did that feel?
- After reading this passage, how do you feel about God?
- Whatever your reactions or questions, you can talk them over with God. After you have your say, just be quiet for a while and notice what happens. Often when we talk to God, we don't wait to see if there is a response. Let God have a chance to get in a word too.

Perhaps some of my own reactions put as questions may help you. Did you notice how often the text reads "And God said"? God speaks, and the whole vast world comes into being and slowly evolves into its present form. There is no hint of exertion on God's part; what God wants comes into existence with a word. It's as if God were playfully allowing imagination to take over: "What about clouds? What about winds? Why not birds and lions and dogs and cats? And snakes, mosquitoes, ants, etc.?" How do you respond to such an image of God creating?

Also, notice how often we hear, "And God saw that it was good." The writer is emphasizing the goodness of creation as it comes from God's hands. Don't you sense that God is having a great time? Does this prayerful reading bring you closer to God? Do you like what you are experiencing? Notice what you are feeling, thinking, and experiencing and tell God about what you notice. Then wait to see how God might respond.

Ask God to help you have a sense of the greatness, might, and total otherness of God. Let it sink in that, with a word, God creates and keeps this vast universe, with its billions of galaxies and eons of time, in existence. In The Wisdom of Solomon the author tells God, "For you love all things that exist, / and detest none of the things that you have made, / for you would not have made anything if you had hated it. . . . You spare all things, for they are yours, O Lord, you who love the living" (Wisdom 11:24, 26). A Portuguese translation I once read translates the last words, *amigo da vida*, "friend of life." That biblical author, writing in Greek under the pseudonym of King Solomon, declares that love motivates God in creation, love of everything that exists.

A reminder: Is it time to take a break from reading and prayer? When you return to the book and to prayer, remember the suggestions for beginning a period of prayer or prayerful reading.

God's act of creation is not a one-and-done thing; it is ongoing. We experience that creative act of God with every breath we take. God is always with us because, in creation, God is always working out the divine purpose or intention. But we are mostly unaware of God's presence and of the fact that we exist at all times because God *keeps* creating. People have, however, felt that creative presence of God in nature. I suggest that on some fine morning, you ask God's help to experience that creative presence. Then step outside and enjoy the day. Sense the sun on your body, smell the air, feel the breezes.

God's Love Beats at the Heart of the Universe

Once, while pondering a homily on the love of God, I thought of how the whole world beats, as it were, with the love of God, who creates out of love and who is love: "God is love, and those who abide in love abide in God, and God abides in them" (1 John 4:16). God is love, nothing but love. Then I thought of the very last words of *The Divine Comedy*.

Here my powers rest from their high fantasy,
    but already I could feel my being turned—
    instinct and intellect balanced equally
as in a wheel whose motions nothing jars—
    by the Love that moves the Sun and the other stars.
      (p. 894)

A lovely image! Dante comes to the end of his long journey through hell, purgatory, and paradise and finds himself inexorably attracted to God. As a sunflower slowly moves with the sun, so Dante's whole being is drawn toward God. Everything that exists, Dante is saying, is drawn by this love, himself included. Isn't that amazing?

> Allow yourself to be drawn by the love that moves the sun and the other stars, the sunflowers, the plants, everything. At the core of the universe, you might say, is the heart of God beating with love for everything created, keeping everything in existence and drawing everything toward God's dream. You could ask God to help you to sense and believe that you are the object of God's great love, compassion, and joy.

If we can get an inkling of how these two truths—absolute otherness and greatness *and* tender love and care for each one of us—coexist in God, then we cannot fail to be attracted to

God and want to love God with our whole heart and mind and soul.

As you ponder the words of Genesis and let them sink in, tell God whatever you are feeling. Before we move on to the next section of Genesis 1, you may want to go back over the first 25 verses of Genesis once or twice more. Take your time. Repetition of prayer periods can enhance their impact as we grow closer to God. Remember that you are asking God for a favor, to grasp as fully as you can the wonders of creation so that you will be filled with the love of a God who loves the world and you so much.

St. Francis of Assisi wrote a lovely canticle of praise, urging all creatures to praise God. The popular hymn "All Creatures of Our God and King" is based on that canticle. You might be helped to express your feelings about God by singing that hymn.

> All creatures of our God and King,
> Lift up your voice and with us sing
> Alleluia! Alleluia!
> Thou burning sun with golden beam,
> Thou silver moon with softer gleam,
> O praise Him, O praise Him,
> Alleluia, alleluia, alleluia!
>
> Thou rushing wind that are so strong,
> Ye clouds that sail in heav'n along,

O praise Him, Alleluia!
Thou rising morn in praise rejoice,
Ye lights of evening, find a voice,
O praise Him, O praise Him,
Alleluia, alleluia, alleluia!

Thou flowing water, pure and clear,
Make music for thy Lord to hear,
Alleluia, Alleluia!
Thou fire so masterful and bright,
That givest man both warmth and light,
O praise Him, O praise Him,
Alleluia, alleluia, alleluia!

And all ye men of tender heart,
Forgiving others, take your part
O sing ye, Alleluia!
Ye who long pain and sorrow bear,
Praise God and on Him cast your care,
O praise Him, O praise Him,
Alleluia, alleluia, alleluia!

Let all things their Creator bless,
And worship Him in humbleness,
O praise Him, Alleluia!
Praise, praise the Father, praise the Son,
And praise the Spirit, three in one,

O praise Him, O praise Him,
Alleluia, alleluia, alleluia!

A reminder: Is it time to take a break from reading and prayer? When you return to the book and to prayer, remember the suggestions for beginning a period of prayer or prayerful reading.

The Creation Story, Part 2:
God Chose to Rely on Us

When you are ready to move on to the creation of human beings, continue reading the rest of the first chapter of Genesis. Remember the suggestions for beginning a period of prayer. When you're ready, read the rest of this first creation tradition slowly and prayerfully. It begins at Genesis 1:26 and ends at Genesis 2:3. After you have finished reading to your satisfaction, return to the paragraphs below.

How did this section strike you? Was there anything that caused you to pause and wonder? Did you have, even momentarily, a sense of God being with you as you read? Tell God about all that you experienced as you read and see if you and God begin some sort of conversation.

> What is the most remarkable thing about this passage? Think about it for a moment before going on to read how I answer the question.

For me, the most striking and awe-inspiring part of this story is that God makes human beings in God's own image and likeness; we are made *like* God. It's remarkable indeed. Of course, God has no other model than Godself in creating the whole universe. Thus, in a sense, everything created is in God's image. But the writer of Genesis means more than this because he makes this point twice. Of no other creature does he write that it is made in the image and likeness of God. Something special is going on here, something upon which we need to reflect and pray, over and over. We human beings, with all our flaws, all our pettiness, all our frailties, all our sinfulness, all our weakness, nonetheless are made in the image and likeness of God in some way that distinguishes us from the rest of creation. What is different about us? You might want to talk with God about this, asking what God had in mind.

The Humility of God

Earlier we saw that love seems to be what moves God to create the universe. It seems to me that, in creating human beings in God's own image and likeness, God's love reaches an apex. You will have noticed that human beings are given "dominion" over the rest of creation. I know that environmentalists are horrified by this, sometimes seeming to blame God or the writer of Genesis for the results of our dominion over creation. But perhaps their blame is misplaced.

True enough, we have made a mess of our planet and are now in the process of polluting outer space with our garbage. However, we need to read this section of Genesis in relation to the whole chapter and especially in relation to the fact that we are made in the image and likeness of God. God is giving us an opportunity *to work with God in building up creation*; God asks us human images to be images of God in our use of the resources put at our disposal in creation.

Here is where we can be struck with awe at the depth and height and length of God's love for us. God wants us to be like God in the way we take care of one another and take care of the rest of creation. In effect, this is a sign of God's humility. God wants a world in which we humans live in harmony and friendship with God, with one another, and with the whole of creation. But God cannot have what God wants without our cooperation. Because we have minds and free wills, we may—or may not—choose to live as images and likenesses of God in this world. So, in a sense, God's dream for our world depends on our choice, on how we live and act. Unfortunately for ourselves and for our world, too often we have not chosen wisely and have acted inhumanely—that is, acted against our nature as creatures made in God's image.

Let it sink in, the kind of other-directed love God expresses by creating us to be God's images, God's stand-ins, as it were, in this created universe. God relies on how we use the gifts God has given us. That's how unselfish God's love is. God creates a universe in which much of what God wants to happen depends on us. God relies on us that much; God loves us and trusts us that much. And God keeps on creating us and sustaining us in existence even though we so very often fail to live and act as images of God and thus make a mess of God's good creation.

At the end of his *Spiritual Exercises*, Ignatius of Loyola suggests a "Contemplation for Attaining Love for God." We will look at this exercise in more detail later. But, before he gets into the suggestions for the contemplation itself, Ignatius writes something that is pertinent to our present topic of God's humility: "It will be good to notice two things at the start: (i) love ought to find its expression in deeds more than in words; (ii) love consists in mutual communication, i.e., the lover gives and communicates to the beloved whatever the lover has, or something of what the lover has or is able to give, and the beloved in turn does the same for the lover. Thus one who possesses knowledge will give it to the one without it, and similarly the possessor of honour or wealth shares with the one who lacks these, each giving to the other" (*Sp. Ex.* 230).

The first point is no surprise: love is shown "in deeds more than in words." In fact, one could say the same thing about faith. "Faith is shown in deeds more than in words." Both love and faith are more like verbs than nouns. They reveal their presence by our actions much more than by our words. It's the second point that deserves comment. In it Ignatius proposes that God wants mutuality between God and us. God wants something from us. What can we give God that God does not have? What do you think? Isn't it that God wants our trust, our love, our friendship, which can only be freely given? Imagine that! God, who needs nothing, wants our trust, our love, and our friendship. It gives God pleasure, you might say, when we trust God, tell God our secrets, our dreams, our hopes, and when we love God with all our heart, and with all our soul, and with all our mind, and with all our strength. This is God's humility: God wants my trust, my love, my friendship. That's mind-boggling! Doesn't it make God more loveable?

In "Hurrahing in Harvest," Gerard Manley Hopkins, SJ, writes about the land at harvesttime. Then suddenly he becomes aware of all the beauty around him: "These things, these things were here and but the beholder wanting." All these beautiful things were there before this moment, but he, in a sense, was not. With that shift he becomes the beholder who was needed. If we could behold the world in this way, we would be contemplatives in action, and we would be aware of God's loving presence at all times.

The Invisible Web of Love

Consider this, from Robert Ellsberg's *The Saints' Guide to Happiness*. The image he uses may remind you, as it did me, of the lines from Dante cited earlier in this session.

> We know that we are surrounded at all times by forces that remain invisible to our unassisted eyes: ultraviolet rays from the sun, electromagnetic waves, radio signals or television images, the conversations that bounce between cellular phones. If some tincture could render these waves and forces visible, we would find ourselves swimming in a sea of light, color, and sound, all dimensions of a reality that forms no part of our normal perception or consciousness.
>
> The saints were attuned to a similar invisible reality: the fact that we all are connected in a web of love and that the universe is rooted and sustained in a reality that,

if we had eyes to see, would at once astonish and awaken us from the dream of separateness.

Ellsberg then goes on to tell the story of a young Catholic priest, Engelmar Unzeitig, who was a Nazi prisoner in the Dachau concentration camp near Munich. When there was an outbreak of typhoid in the camp, all those who were infected were put into one barrack. When a call went out for volunteers to take care of the victims of typhoid fever, he was one of twenty priests to step forward. Within a short time, he had the fever and died a few weeks before the liberation of the camp by Allied troops. He wrote a letter before his death in which he said, among other things,

> The Good is undying and victory must remain with God, even if it sometimes seems useless for us to spread love in the world. Nevertheless, one sees again and again that *the human heart is attuned to love, and it cannot withstand its power in the long run, if it is truly based on God and not on creatures.* We want to continue to do and offer everything so that love and peace may soon reign again. (pp. 100–102, emphasis in original)

Love is at the heart of creation. God's heart, we might say, is beating with love at every moment of this universe's existence. We can ask God to help us be attuned to these invisible rays of love that pulsate from the creative and loving heart of God.

An Evening Prayer

Just as I suggested a morning prayer earlier, let me now suggest an evening prayer.

> Some evening when the sky is clear, go outside and look up at the stars and listen to the sounds around you. Ask God to help you experience his creative love at the heart of everything you sense. At the end, when you return to your own place, you might want to pray/sing "Day Is Done, but Love Unfailing Dwells Ever Here," a hymn that uses a traditional Welsh melody. The words are by James Quinn, SJ, and the hymn is sung at Evening Prayer for Week II of *The Liturgy of Hours*. If you google the title, you'll find a link to the words and also to some sung versions.

PART 2

"I AM . . . THE GOD OF ABRAHAM, THE GOD OF ISAAC, AND THE GOD OF JACOB."

We don't often think of the Old Testament as inspiring us to love; we tend to think of it as a book of history and rules. But I'd like to challenge that perception.

Christians need to remember that the collection of books we call the Old Testament is not old to the Jewish people for whom it was first compiled and that Jews find it offensive for us to refer to their Bible in this way. Moreover, we must never forget that it was the only Bible Jesus knew and the only Bible the early Christians knew until near the end of the first century after Jesus. Finally, we must never forget that the meaning of what we call the New Testament cannot be grasped fully without knowing how our Christian stories were influenced by this collection of books.

We have already used the first chapter of Genesis to inspire our love for God. That chapter begins the story of God's relationship with us humans, and a long story it is, much of it lost in prehistory. Indeed, the story placed in the first chapter of Genesis is part of that prehistory. When the Israelites began to write down the stories that had accumulated about their own origins as a people, one thing was central to their sense of who they were: the one God who had created the world had chosen them to be a special people, not just for their sake but also for the sake of the world. In a sense, the stories that precede the call of Abram and Sarai in chapter 12 of Genesis explain why the good world God had created "in the beginning" was in such a mess that God had to intervene and call a special people.

Recall the image of the Bible as being like a five-act Shakespearean play. In the first act, the world, as it comes from God's hands, is good. Humans introduce disharmony into this world by not living as the images of God they are created to be, the beginning of the second act. The story of humans eating fruit from the tree of good and evil in chapter 3 is the Israelites' way of explaining what has gone wrong with God's good creation. In that chapter, human beings choose not to trust God but to try to control their destiny on their own. The following chapters to the end of chapter 11 depict the results of the original human folly. At the beginning of chapter 11, the loss of a common language is explained as God's punishment because humans had built the tower of Babel. The rest of that chapter gives the genealogy leading to the birth of Abram.

In the third act, something new is introduced to the story of God's relationship with us when, in chapter 12, we read that God calls Abram with his wife Sarai to leave their homeland and travel to "the land that I will show you" (Genesis 12:1). They obey this call without question, pack up everything, and go into an unknown future. Thus begins the story of how God became the "God of Abraham, the God of Isaac, and the God of Jacob," the story of God's relationship with a particular people that ultimately leads to Jesus of Nazareth.

It would be impossible here to go through that whole history. What I want to do is suggest to you some of the salient events and experiences of the history of God's covenant relationship with the people of Israel that, I hope, will help you grow in love for God and for God's ways with us.

As you read these stories of the Israelites, try to get a sense of how the characters react to God's intervention in their lives. Remember that though they are living thousands of years before you, they are still human and have similar reactions to your own. Notice where their story intersects with yours or with the story of someone you know or have heard of. In this way you will find that you have a good deal in common with them and also have more to talk over with God than you first suspected. These stories still touch the lives of people like you and me even after all these years and so many cultural changes.

God of Abraham and Sarah: Promise, Laughter, and Shrewd Negotiations

First, we look at some passages from the story of Abram and Sarai. However, to get the whole picture of this story, you might want to read chapters 12–24 sometime. You will see that Abram and Sarai are real human beings with flaws, foibles, and sins. They are not the kind of people we usually associate with sanctity. For example, in chapter 20 Abram is so afraid for his life that he tells King Abimelech that Sarai is his sister. As a result, she is taken by the king, probably as part of his harem. She is saved only by God's intervention. Later, Sarai forces Abram to send Sarai's maid Hagar out into the desert with her son Ishmael, where they would have died except for God's intervention. These are real human beings like us. Yet God wants their friendship and their cooperation in the great work begun with creation, just as God wants our friendship and cooperation in this great work.

As we begin, remember the suggestions for beginning any reading or prayer session.

I have been using the names Abram and Sarai up to this point, although we know them as Abraham and Sarah. As their friendship with God developed, God gave them these new names. You might almost think of the change as the giving of nicknames, a sign of deeper friendship.

Have you ever wondered if God has a special name for you? Perhaps you can ask God.

Jesus, by the way, seems to have used nicknames for his closest friends, and some of those names probably were humorous at the time. He calls Simon "Peter," which, according to the late Daniel Harrington, could be translated as "Rocky." I've often wondered if Jesus nicknamed James and John "Sons of Thunder" in a humorous reference to how their father Zebedee reacted when James and John were pulled out of the family fishing business to join Jesus.

Humor also emerges as Abraham and Sarah grow more comfortable with God, and sometimes God joins in the humor. Here are some examples.

Abram and Sarai seem to obey without hesitation or question the initial call to leave their homeland. Gradually Abram becomes more daring with God. In Genesis 15, God had promised that Sarai would bear a son from whom would come a people as numerous as the stars. However, Sarai remains barren. So, in chapter 16, Sarai proposes to Abram that he take her maid Hagar to have a son with her. This he does, and Hagar gives birth to Ishmael. In chapter 17, when Abram is 99 and Sarai 89, God again speaks to him, introduces the covenant ritual of circumcision, and changes Abram's name to Abraham and Sarai to Sarah. God tells Abraham that he will have a son by Sarah. At this point we read,

> Then Abraham fell on his face and laughed, and said to himself, "Can a child be born to a man who is a hundred years old? Can Sarah, who is ninety years old, bear a child?" And Abraham said to God, "O that Ishmael might live in your sight!" God said, "No, but your wife Sarah shall bear you a son, and you shall name him Isaac [meaning 'Laughter']. I will establish my covenant with him as an everlasting covenant for his offspring after him. As for Ishmael, I have heard you; I will bless him and make him fruitful and exceedingly numerous. . . . But my covenant I will establish with Isaac, whom Sarah shall bear to you at this season next year." And when he had finished

talking with him, God went up from Abraham. (Genesis 17:17–22)

In this little story, Abraham falls down in laughter at the idea that he and Sarah could have a son at their age and, basically, tells God to be serious and bless Ishmael. God gets into the humorous spirit by giving the son to come the name "Laughter" and telling Abraham, "but I heard you and will bless Ishmael." It's the kind of humorous conversation good friends have.

Then in chapter 18 the Lord appears to Abraham again at his camp in the desert. In this scene God is sometimes "the LORD," sometimes "three men." This blurring of the line between God and angels seems to be characteristic of the original writer of this chapter. It is not a veiled reference to the Christian doctrine of the Trinity. I take it that God's presence is meant in this chapter. At any rate, Abraham treats his visitor(s) with usual Middle Eastern hospitality. Sarah prepares a meal for them, and after they have eaten, we read,

They [the three] said to him, "Where is your wife, Sarah?" And he said, "There, in the tent." Then one said, "I will surely return to you in due season, and your wife Sarah shall have a son." And Sarah was listening at the tent entrance behind him. Now Abraham and Sarah were old, advanced in age; it had ceased to be with Sarah after the manner of women. So Sarah laughed to herself, saying,

"After I have grown old, and my husband is old, shall I have pleasure?" The LORD said to Abraham, "Why did Sarah laugh, and say, 'Shall I indeed bear a child, now that I am old?' Is anything too wonderful for the LORD? At the set time I will return to you, in due season, and Sarah shall have a son." But Sarah denied, saying, "I did not laugh"; for she was afraid. He said, "Oh yes, you did laugh." (Genesis 18:9–15)

How do you react to these stories? Did you laugh or at least smile at times? Have you ever been as honest and direct with God as Abraham and Sarah are? Would you like to be able to be this way with God? With what tone of voice did you hear God say, "As for Ishmael, I have heard you"? Or "Oh yes, you did"? I felt that God spoke in a humorous way, e.g., to Abraham: "Okay, I get your humor; I'll take care of Ishmael, but old as you are, you and Sarah will have a child." Are you enjoying God more, feeling more able to love God? You may want to have a conversation with God about this story and about your own reactions and the desires the story evokes in you.

Is it time to take a break? If you do so, remember the suggestions about how to begin any period of prayer or reading when you return to the book.

Telling God How to Be God

Immediately after the last scene we considered, God leaves to see whether things are as bad in Sodom and Gomorrah as reported. Abraham starts out with God, and God ruminates, "Shall I hide from Abraham what I am about to do, seeing that Abraham will become a great and mighty nation, and all the nations of the earth shall be blessed in him? No, for I have chosen him. . . ." (Genesis 18:17–19). God tells Abraham that he intends to destroy Sodom and Gomorrah if they are as evil as reported. Abraham then speaks up and tells God what he thinks of this intended action. He's amazing in his bluntness and honesty, which lead to this dialogue:

> "Will you indeed sweep away the righteous with the wicked? Suppose there are fifty righteous within the city; will you then sweep away the place and not forgive it for the fifty righteous who are in it? Far be it from you to do such a thing, to slay the righteous with the wicked, so that the righteous fare as the wicked! Far be that from you! Shall not the Judge of all the earth do what is just?" And the LORD said, "If I find at Sodom fifty righteous in the city, I will forgive the whole place for their sake." Abraham answered, "Let me take it upon myself to speak to the Lord, I who am but dust and ashes. Suppose five of the fifty righteous are lacking? Will you destroy the whole city for lack of five?" And he said, "I will not destroy it if I find forty-five there." Again he spoke to him, "Suppose

forty are found there." He answered, "For the sake of forty I will not do it." Then he said, "Oh do not let the Lord be angry if I speak. Suppose thirty are found there." He answered, "I will not do it, if I find thirty there." He said, "Let me take it upon myself to speak to the Lord. Suppose twenty are found there." He answered, "For the sake of twenty I will not destroy it." Then he said, "Oh do not let the Lord be angry if I speak just once more. Suppose ten are found there." He answered, "For the sake of ten I will not destroy it." And the LORD went his way, when he had finished speaking to Abraham; and Abraham returned to his place. (Genesis 18:23–33)

It's a great story, isn't it? Of course, no one was there taking dictation, but there must have been a tradition that Abraham tried to prevent the destruction of Sodom and Gomorrah by bargaining with God. And the writer felt that the kind of friendship Abraham had with God deserved a funny, yet serious, story that would remind anyone who heard it of the kind of haggling that still goes on in the marketplaces of the Middle East and elsewhere. Did you cringe at all when Abraham began his intervention? I do, almost instinctively, when I hear him tell God how to be God. Would you like to have this kind of friendship with God, the kind that would let you easily slip into banter and even harsh remonstrance with God on occasion? Well, the way to have such a relationship is to engage regularly with God. Over time you will find yourself changing in the way you relate to God.

Have you ever felt that God had dealt you, or someone you love, very bad and undeserved cards? Did you or do you wish you could have spoken as openly and honestly with God about your feelings as Abraham did in this story? Do you feel more attracted to God after this prayerful reflection? Do you love God more? Take some time to speak with God about your reactions to these passages.

A reminder: You may want to take a break from reading and praying at this time. When you are ready, continue to the next section.

God, Moses, and Face-to-Face Friendship

Genesis ends with the twelve sons of Jacob and their families, servants, and livestock going to Egypt because of a famine. There they are saved from famine because one of Jacob's sons, Joseph, whom his ten older brothers had sold into slavery, ended up as the Egyptian pharaoh's right-hand man and the distributor of grain to Egyptians as well as to refugees such as his brothers. The next book of the Bible, Exodus, tells the story of the later enslavement of the Israelites by the Egyptians and their being saved by God under the leadership of Moses. There are a couple of stories of God's self-revelation to Moses that might remind you of some aspect of your relationship with God and be helpful to you for prayer. As we begin this section, I remind you of the suggestions for beginning every period of reading and/or of prayer.

The section of Exodus I suggest for your prayer contains the great revelation to Moses of God's name, YHWH. Remember what I said earlier about how God changed the names of Abram and Sarai, indicating a new depth of friendship with them. Here God gives Moses, and thus all the Israelites, God's holy name. It indicates, on God's part, an act of unparalleled intimacy and love. The Israelites had such reverence for this name that they often did not say it aloud and developed other names for God. You may have noticed that Jews sometimes write *G-D* when they want to mention the name in English. In the New Revised Standard Version translation, the presence of the name YHWH is indicated this way: LORD.

In this story, you will notice that God's appearance to Moses is motivated by the suffering of the Israelites. God is moved by compassion for the suffering of his people to save them from their enslavement and bring them to the land promised to Abraham, Isaac, and Jacob. A prominent rabbi, Abba bar Mammal, in the early centuries after the birth of Jesus wrote that God said to Moses that he will be known as YHWH when he shows compassion for the world. The Hebrew word translated "compassion" has resonances with the word for *womb*; God has a "womb-love" for his people. This Hebrew word "compassion" becomes, from the time of this revelation, almost a definition of who God is. Rabbi Abba bar Mammal lived in the late third century / early fourth century after the birth of Jesus. For more on his reading of the revelation at the burning bush, see Oliver Davies, *A Theology of Compassion: Metaphysics of Difference and the Renewal of Tradition*, 243.

Moses, in self-imposed exile from Egypt, was in Midian, where he tended the flocks of his father-in-law. One day near Horeb, the mountain of the Lord, Moses noticed a bush burning that was not consumed by the fire and decided to approach to see what was up. The story continues:

> When the Lord saw that he had turned aside to see, God called to him out of the bush, "Moses, Moses!" And he said, "Here I am." Then he said, "Come no closer! Remove the sandals from your feet, for the place on which you are standing is holy ground." He said further, "I am the God of your father, the God of Abraham, the God of Isaac, and the God of Jacob." And Moses hid his face, for he was afraid to look at God.
>
> Then the Lord said, "I have observed the misery of my people who are in Egypt; I have heard their cry on account of their taskmasters. Indeed, I know their sufferings, and I have come down to deliver them from the Egyptians, and to bring them up out of that land to a good and broad land, a land flowing with milk and honey. . . . So come, I will send you to Pharaoh to bring my people, the

Israelites, out of Egypt." But Moses said to God, "Who am I that I should go to Pharaoh, and bring the Israelites out of Egypt?" He said, "I will be with you; and this shall be the sign for you that it is I who sent you: when you have brought the people out of Egypt, you shall worship God on this mountain."

But Moses said to God, "If I come to the Israelites and say to them, 'The God of your ancestors has sent me to you,' and they ask me, 'What is his name?' what shall I say to them"? God said to Moses, "I AM WHO I AM." He said further, "Thus you shall say to the Israelites, 'I AM has sent me to you.'" God also said to Moses, "Thus you shall say to the Israelites, 'The LORD, the God of your ancestors, the God of Abraham, the God of Isaac, and the God of Jacob, has sent me to you':

This is my name for ever,
and this my title for all generations." (Exodus 3:4–15)

Did the passage capture your imagination and cause some reactions? Did you want to run away from the bush? Toward it? What did you feel as you read? Were you attracted to God?

Did you notice that God was motivated by compassion or womb-love for the Israelites? Have you ever experienced something like God's compassion for you? How did you feel toward God?

Did you wonder how you would have responded if you had been Moses? Did it occur to you that God might have something to ask you? How would you feel if God did speak directly to you and made a request of you?

Do you sense yourself growing in love for God? Have you noticed in yourself a greater ease in listening and speaking to God? Have you noticed yourself thinking more about God during the day as you engage in this kind of prayer? Your answers to such questions may give you things to talk over with God.

"Show Me Yourself"

Moses, obviously, accepted God's challenging call. After many plagues, the pharaoh finally gave in and let the Israelites leave Egypt with all their cattle and goods. From Egypt the Israelites went into the Sinai desert, where they had many encounters with God and often angered God with their infidelities and complaining. At one point, Moses spent forty days alone with God on Mount Sinai, where God gave him two tablets with the Ten Commandments written on them. Tired of waiting for Moses to come down, the people asked Moses' brother, Aaron, to make for them a golden calf, which they began to worship. God was ready to destroy them completely and start over again with Moses, but Moses intervened, reminding God of his promises to Abraham, Isaac, and Jacob, and God relented (Exodus 32:11–14). In Exodus 33:11 we read, "Thus the LORD used to speak to Moses face to face, as one speaks to a friend." Moses has become very familiar with God. Right after this statement, we are presented with some scenes that show God's great love for Moses and for the Israelites. You may want to use these stories for prayer.

> Moses said to the LORD, "See, you have said to me, 'Bring up this people'; but you have not let me know whom you will send with me. Yet you have said, 'I know you by name, and you have also found favor in my sight.' Now if I have found favor in your sight, show me your ways, so that I may know you and find favor in your sight. Consider too that this nation is your people." He said, "My presence will go with you, and I will give you rest." And he said to him, "If your presence will not go, do not carry us up from here. For how shall it be known that I have found favor in your sight, I and your people, unless you go with us? In this way, we shall be distinct, I and your people, from every people on the face of the earth."
>
> The LORD said to Moses, "I will do the very thing that you have asked; for you have found favor in my sight, and I know you by name." (Exodus 33:12–17)

Moses went up Mount Sinai the next morning and stood where God told him to stand.

The LORD descended in the cloud and stood with him there, and proclaimed the name, "The LORD." The LORD passed before him, and proclaimed,

> "The LORD, the LORD,
> a God merciful and gracious,
> slow to anger,
> and abounding in steadfast love and faithfulness,
> keeping steadfast love for the thousandth generation,
> forgiving iniquity and transgression and sin,
> yet by no means clearing the guilty,
> but visiting the iniquity of the parents
> upon the children
> and the children's children,
> to the third and the fourth generation."

And Moses quickly bowed his head towards the earth, and worshiped. He said, "If now I have found favor in your sight, O Lord, I pray, let the Lord go with us. Although this is a stiff-necked people, pardon our iniquity and our sin, and take us for your inheritance." (Exodus 34:5–9)

God then renewed the covenant with the Israelites.

Along with the revelation of God's name at the burning bush, this passage was central to the Israelites' understanding of who God is and how God wants to be known. Parts of this revelation are cited many times in the Bible, for example, Numbers 14:18; Deuteronomy 5:9–10; Psalms 86:15 and 145:8–9; Jeremiah 32:18; Joel 2:13; Jonah 4:2; and

Nahum 1:3. That will give you some idea of how it resonated in the hearts and memories of the Israelites. Remember that God is the Creator of the universe, the Mystery beyond our comprehension and understanding, the completely Other before whom all that is created is, as Julian of Norwich saw, as insignificant as a hazelnut. This mysterious other speaks with Moses, a human being like us, "face to face, as one speaks to a friend" (Exodus 33:11). God becomes that vulnerable, wanting Moses' friendship, knowing that Moses can refuse the offer. God continues to love these Israelites who are as faithless, small-minded, petty, and self-serving as we can be.

How do you react to these scenes? Did you notice how cheeky Moses was in asking God to show his face? Could you speak to God that way? Would you want to be that comfortable with God to be able to speak that way? (I hope that you are becoming more comfortable as your reading and praying progress.)

Did you notice that Moses gives God two motivations for granting his request: God's own promises to Moses and God's covenant relationship with the Israelites? "You told me that I had found favor with you, and these are your people." Moses is holding God to his promises to himself and to Israel. Moses sounds as comfortable with God as Abraham was when he told God how to be God before the destruction of Sodom and Gomorrah, doesn't he?

I have asked God to awe me with his presence, as he awed Moses. I have had only inklings of how awesome God is. I keep asking for this grace, but I know that the grace is totally up to God. There is nothing I can do to make myself feel such awe. You may be in the same boat. It's a good reminder to us that God alone is God and that we have no control over how God will respond. The only honest and realistic stance is to appear before God, hat in hand, as it were, asking for what we want. Of course, that's what we have been doing throughout the prayers of this book.

You might reflect on some information about words God speaks to Moses. God uses the name YHWH given to Moses at the burning bush. The words "a God merciful and gracious, slow to anger, and abounding in steadfast love and faithfulness" appear over and over again throughout the Hebrew Bible. The Hebrew word translated "merciful" by the NRSV is *racham*, which many think is best translated as "compassion" and which, as noted, is related to the word for womb. The Hebrew word translated as "steadfast love" is *hesed*, sometimes written *chesid*, and is associated with God's covenant love. Finally, the Hebrew word translated "faithfulness" is *emet* and connotes God's reliability or fidelity to the covenant. God is moved by womb-love in relating to the Israelites and to us, and God, as it were, makes a blood oath of steadfast love and fidelity to them and to us. How do you react to that?

You may be put off by the threat contained in the last words of that revelation. Remember, however, that God does have standards; no one can be in God's presence without experiencing how far he or she is from being an image of God. At the same time, we must never forget that God's judgment is always contained within God's mercy and love. God is not in a zero-sum game with us; with God, love is always the first and last word. As Michael Himes said, in a class at Boston College, "the least wrong way to imagine God . . . is to think of God as love." Note, too, that God's covenant love is guaranteed to the thousandth generation, which means forever, while the judgment against iniquity lasts only to the third and fourth generation. In addition, I once heard that a man told Fr. J. Bryan Hehir, of the Boston Archdiocese, of his trouble holding together God's mercy and justice, to which Fr. Hehir replied, "But remember that it's no problem for God." The Bible is often self-correcting; what is said in one passage may be changed in a later passage of the Bible. Perhaps it was the threat of punishment of children and grandchildren for the sins of their ancestors that led to the saying cited in Jeremiah:

In those days they shall no longer say:

"The parents have eaten sour grapes,
    and the children's teeth are set on edge.

But all shall die for their own sins; the teeth of everyone who eats sour grapes shall be set on edge." (Jeremiah 31:29–30)

In other words, here Jeremiah has God changing that saying.

Are you feeling more warmth and love for God as a result of praying with this revelation? You may want to tell God what you are feeling. If you are still feeling great fear of God's judgment, you can talk to God about your feelings and ask for God's response.

A reminder: Take a break if you have been reading or praying for too long. When you are ready, you can look at the next suggestion to see if it will help you to love God more. Remember the suggestions about how to begin any period of reading and/or prayer.

God Keeps Loving
Wayward People

Rather oddly for the founding history of a people, the Bible says very little about how heroic the Israelites' ancestors were; more often we read of their failures. All their great heroes have feet of clay, and the people themselves continually fail in their covenant relationship with their God. But God continues to be faithful to them. For example, in the desert, after God has rescued them from slavery and given them manna and quail to eat, the Israelites grumble, "If only we had meat to eat! We remember the fish we used to eat in Egypt for nothing, the cucumbers, the melons, the leeks, the onions, and the garlic; but now our strength is dried up and there is nothing at all but this manna to look at" (Numbers 11:4–6); David, easily their greatest king, is depicted as an adulterer who murders one of his soldiers because he (David) has impregnated the man's wife; God repeatedly sends prophets to try to bring the Israelites back to their senses, and, most often, they fail to follow the prophets' advice. This foundation history is one of infidelity and sin on the part of the Israelites, and unbelievable forbearance and forgiveness on the part of God.

In this section, I suggest looking at some passages that illustrate this aspect of God's dealings with the Israelites in the hope that a prayerful reflection on them will help you grow in your comprehension of God's love. Remember the suggestions for beginning each session of prayer or reading.

We have already looked at how God forgave the Israelites, at Moses' insistence, after they had forced Aaron to make a golden calf. During the period when the Babylonians threatened the Israelites in Jerusalem, Jeremiah was sent as a reluctant prophet to tell them to make peace with this overwhelming force rather than to trust in an alliance with Egypt. The leaders and many of the people refused to heed him and treated him quite badly, even threatening him with death. The disasters Jeremiah predicted if they did not heed his words came to pass: Jerusalem was sacked, the temple destroyed, and many of the leading citizens, artisans, and skilled workers were taken into exile in Babylon. This was the greatest calamity in Israel's history; it appeared that God had given up on them. At that time, Jeremiah was told to write down God's promises of forgiveness and restitution to the land. Let's read prayerfully the following passages:

At that time, says the LORD, I will be the God of all the families of Israel, and they shall be my people.

Thus says the LORD:
The people who survived the sword
   found grace in the wilderness;
when Israel sought for rest,
   the LORD appeared to him, from far away.
I have loved you with an everlasting love;
   therefore I have continued my faithfulness to you.
Again I will build you, and you shall be built,
   O virgin Israel! (Jeremiah 31:1–4)

Hear the word of the LORD, O nations,
   and declare it in the coastlands far away;
say, "He who scattered Israel will gather him,
   and will keep him as a shepherd a flock."
For the LORD has ransomed Jacob,
   and has redeemed him from hands too strong
      for him.
They shall come and sing aloud on the height of Zion,
   and they shall be radiant over the goodness of the
      LORD,
over the grain, the wine, and the oil,
   and over the young of the flock and the herd;
their life shall become like a watered garden,

> and they shall never languish again.
> Then shall the young women rejoice in the dance,
>   and the young men and the old shall be merry.
> I will turn their mourning into joy,
>   I will comfort them, and give them gladness for
>   sorrow. (Jeremiah 31:10–13)

The days are surely coming, says the LORD, when I will make a new covenant with the house of Israel and the house of Judah. It will not be like the covenant that I made with their ancestors when I took them by the hand to bring them out of the land of Egypt—a covenant that they broke, though I was their husband, says the LORD. But this is the covenant that I will make with the house of Israel after those days, says the LORD: I will put my law within them, and I will write it on their hearts; and I will be their God, and they shall be my people. No longer shall they teach one another, or say to each other, "Know the LORD," for they shall all know me, from the least of them to the greatest, says the LORD; for I will forgive their iniquity, and remember their sin no more. (Jeremiah 31:31–34)

Have you ever felt that you had so deeply offended someone you loved that you thought that person would never forgive you? If so, then you have some idea of what the Israelites must feel before God after this terrible debacle. Yet God tells them, "I have loved you with an everlasting love." "I will never stop loving you; yes, you have sinned and treated me and

Jeremiah very badly, but I forgive you and want to continue our friendship and covenant. Don't be afraid of me." Can you hear God saying these words, or at least the ones that could apply, to you? How do you react to God speaking this way to you? Do you want to talk with God about your reactions? Do you feel more love for such a forgiving, loving God?

While we are on the Babylon debacle, let's look at some passages from what is called Second Isaiah, chapters 40–55 of Isaiah. The first thirty-nine chapters of Isaiah, more or less, were written by the one called First Isaiah during the time just before the Babylonian captivity. Chapters 40–55 were written during the Babylonian captivity, during the seventy or so years the exiles lived as slaves in Babylon. This downtrodden, seemingly forsaken and sinful people hear these words. Let's listen to them prayerfully as a revelation of who God is.

> Comfort, O comfort my people,
>   says your God.
> Speak tenderly to Jerusalem,
>   and cry to her
> that she has served her term,
>   that her penalty is paid,
> that she has received from the LORD's hand
>   double for all her sins.
> A voice cries out:

"In the wilderness prepare the way of the LORD,
    make straight in the desert a highway for our God.
Every valley shall be lifted up,
    and every mountain and hill be made low;
the uneven ground shall become level,
    and the rough places a plain.
Then the glory of the LORD shall be revealed,
    and all people shall see it together,
for the mouth of the LORD has spoken."
(Isaiah 40:1–5)

These words are probably familiar to you because of the opening lines of Handel's *Messiah*.

> Again, imagine those downcast, lost, and exiled Israelites as they hear God's words. God is promising to bring them back through mountains and deserts to the Promised Land. Can you hear God speaking similar words to you? How do you react? You may want to talk to God about your reactions before going on to the next passage.

In Isaiah 43, God speaks very tenderly to this exiled people. If you have ever felt lost and forsaken because of your own moral and human weaknesses, recall that time so that you will be in the frame of mind of the Israelites to whom God speaks through these words of Isaiah.

But now thus says the LORD,
    he who created you, O Jacob,
    he who formed you, O Israel:
Do not fear, for I have redeemed you;
    I have called you by name, you are mine.
When you pass through the waters, I will be with you;
    and through the rivers, they shall not
        overwhelm you;
when you walk through fire you shall not be burned,
    and the flame shall not consume you.
For I am the LORD your God,
    the Holy One of Israel, your Savior.
I give Egypt as your ransom,
    Ethiopia and Seba in exchange for you.
Because you are precious in my sight,
    and honored, and I love you,
I give people in return for you,
    nations in exchange for your life.
Do not fear, for I am with you;
    I will bring your offspring from the east,
    and from the west I will gather you;
I will say to the north, "Give them up,"
    and to the south, "Do not withhold;
bring my sons from far away
    and my daughters from the end of the earth—
everyone who is called by my name,
    whom I created for my glory,
    whom I formed and made." (Isaiah 43:1–7)

Through the great prophet, God is telling this exiled and downtrodden people that they are still the apple of his eye and that he will bring them back from wherever they have been exiled. Why? Just because God loves them.

Can you feel the warmth and tenderness of these words? Can you hear them, at least some of them, as being said by God to you? How do you react? You may want to talk with God about your reactions.

When you are ready, you may want to go on to the last passage from Second Isaiah, this one from chapter 49.

> Sing for joy, O heavens, and exult, O earth;
>   break forth, O mountains, into singing!
> For the LORD has comforted his people,
>   and will have compassion on his suffering ones.
> But Zion said, "The LORD has forsaken me,
>   my Lord has forgotten me."
> Can a woman forget her nursing child,
>   or show no compassion for the child of her womb?
> Even these may forget,
>   yet I will not forget you.
> See, I have inscribed you on the palms of my hands;
>   your walls are continually before me.
> (Isaiah 49:13–16)

I hope you noticed the word *compassion* twice in this tender prophecy. In addition, God is likened to a mother with the child of her womb. What womb-love God expresses for these sinful exiles! Do you hear God speaking to you with such tenderness? Do you want to tell God how you feel?

The great Swiss theologian Karl Barth once wrote: "*Is it true*, this talk of a loving and good God, who is more than one of the friendly idols whose rise is so easy to account for, and whose dominion is so brief? What the people want to find out and thoroughly understand is, *Is it true*?" (emphasis added). Based on my own experience and observation, I agree with Barth. It seems that deep within each of us sits a strong fear that, *at least for me, God is not love, no matter how often I hear it.* I hope that the prayerful reflections of this chapter have eased those deep fears in you as writing and praying them has done in me. I also hope that you are growing in your love for God.

PART 3

THE HUMILITY OF GOD

I want to encourage you to spend more time on the notion of the humility of God as a way to be drawn toward loving God with all your heart, soul, mind, and strength. I hope you will realize that God has, over and over again, gone the extra mile because of love for us; such a realization cannot but increase our desire to love God. As we begin, I remind you of the suggestions about how to begin every period of prayer or even every period of reading this book.

The Word Became Flesh

We have already reflected on God's humility in wanting us as friends and partners in creation. God wants our love and our cooperation in the great work of bringing about what God intends in creating this universe. This is a desire that we can, and often do, refuse.

Well, if we have been awed by such humility, what are we to make of God's *becoming one of us*? The opening lines of John's Gospel evoke the first words of Genesis:

> In the beginning was the Word, and the Word was with God, and the Word was God. He was in the beginning with God. All things came into being through him, and without him not one thing came into being. What has come into being in him was life, and the life was the light of all people. The light shines in the darkness, and the darkness did not overcome it. (John 1:1–5)

John continues this reference to creation when he proclaims, "And the Word became flesh and lived among us, and we have seen his glory, the glory as of a father's only son, full of grace and truth" (John 1:14).

God, the Creator of the universe, has taken on our flesh and has pitched his tent among us (another translation of "lived among us"). What this means is that God, the Creator, becomes one of us, becomes a baby boy who needs the milk of his mother in order to survive, who needs to be toilet trained, to go through the "terrible twos," to be saved from Herod's soldiers as an infant, to be an exile with his mother and father in Egypt, to learn the trade of his father Joseph as a teenager, to figure out his calling in life as a young adult, and so on. God so loves us that he becomes one of us with all that being human entails. "God so loved the world that he gave his only Son, so that everyone who believes in him may not perish but may have eternal life" (John 3:16): that's how humble God is!

Spend some time pondering what you have just read. Notice your reactions and talk with God about them. If you feel more love for God, tell him.

The Age to Come, the Kingdom of God

Remember the suggestions for beginning each period of reading or praying.

Throughout the Bible, God has been promising to set the world to rights in "the age to come." Clearly, the world has been out of joint for as long as humans can remember. The Jewish people, we have seen, were chosen to be God's special people to help God set the world to rights, but they, too, failed to live faithfully as images of God. But throughout their history, God stayed true to his promises that through them, all would be set to rights in "the age to come." This "age to come" will differ from the present age because finally God's dream for creation will be accomplished. Another phrase that evokes this "age to come" is "the new heavens and the new earth." In the Gospels, Jesus often speaks of the "kingdom of God" (in Matthew, "kingdom of heaven"), which I take as referring to the same dream of God for creation.

Over the centuries before the birth of Jesus, the prophets spoke mysteriously of "a son of man" or "the anointed one" (*Messiah* in Hebrew, *Christos* when the Bible was translated into Greek), or a ruler. This figure would usher in "the age to come." Jesus is this mysterious figure. No one could have predicted that the Messiah would actually be God's only Son.

Even more unpredictable, indeed incredible, was what happened to him when he came. Yet that is what we believe is true, that in Jesus, God has come among us as a human being to do for us what we, because of our sins, could not do ourselves. We had failed (and continue to fail) miserably to be the human beings God creates us to be. Yet God decides to become one of us. What seems impossible for us is not impossible for God. Isn't that striking, awe-inspiring? "For God so loved the world that he gave his only Son, so that everyone who believes in him may not perish but may have eternal life" (John 3:16).

> What are your reactions as you ponder these two paragraphs in conjunction with the opening lines of John's Gospel? Do you sense the humility of God, so in love with you and with everyone and everything he has made that he takes the risk of becoming one of us? Maybe you're feeling afraid. If so, do you know what makes you afraid? If you do, tell God and see how the conversation develops. If you are feeling more love for God and more trust in God's friendship, tell him about these reactions and see what develops from there.

The Annunciation

In his *Spiritual Exercises*, Ignatius of Loyola suggests a way of contemplating the Annunciation scene that may help you perceive the humility of God. In Luke 1:26–27 we read, "In the sixth month the angel Gabriel was sent by God to a town in Galilee called Nazareth, to a virgin engaged to a man whose name was Joseph, of the house of David. The virgin's name was Mary." Most of us would focus on the scene with the angel and Mary, but Ignatius imagines the sending of the angel Gabriel by the Trinity. He narrates the story this way: "how the three Divine Persons were looking at all the flatness or roundness of the whole world filled with people, and how the decision was taken in Their eternity, as They saw them all going down into hell, that the second Person would become human to save the human race" (*Sp. Ex.* 102).

Try to imagine this scene. The Trinity, clearly aware of what we have done to this world and to ourselves, clearly aware of how hopelessly lost we are, decides to send the Son to become one of us. Instead of washing their hands of us and giving up the whole enterprise, the Trinity decides to join us in this limited, finite, sinful world and, even more improbably, to die a horrible death on a Roman cross.

After contemplating the Trinity's decision to send the Son, you might want to take up the rest of the story in Luke 1:28–38. I encourage you to open your Bible and read Luke's account.

Let this story grab your imagination. Where are you as you imagine this dialogue? What do you notice about Gabriel's greeting and his attitude toward Mary? How old is Mary? Most commentators believe that she might have been just past the age of puberty, so quite young.

Throughout the centuries, artists have painted this scene, their form of contemplation. Usually they used scenes and models with which they were familiar to depict how the Incarnation touched their hearts and minds. Poets have done the same. You, too, can trust that God will use your imagination to bring home to you what God wants to reveal to you about the Incarnation.

Can you imagine God and the entire heavenly host hanging in suspense, wondering whether Mary will say yes? Well, Mary is free, so God waits on her response. That's how humble God is and how respectful of our freedom! And God, now a fetus, grows in Mary's womb for nine months only to push out of the womb, needing milk and love to live and grow up. God-with-us has to learn how to talk and walk and be toilet trained. Take seriously what it means for God to become a human being. That's how much God loves us!

A reminder: Is it time to take a break from reading and prayer? When you return to the book and/or to prayer, remember the suggestions for beginning a period of prayer or prayerful reading.

John's Prologue

You might also want to reflect in prayer on the opening lines of John's Gospel, asking to grasp with your whole mind, heart, and being the enormity of what God has done in the Incarnation. If you do follow this suggestion, ask God's help to know more intimately God's generous love and humility, then open your Bible to the first chapter of John's Gospel and read verses 1–18 slowly and prayerfully.

How did you react to this reading? What lines particularly struck you? Did you sense the humility of God and, if so, in what way? Your answers to questions like these could lead you to talk to God about your reactions, and this talking might lead to a kind of conversation with God.

By using the phrase *In the beginning*, John wants to remind his readers of the first creation story in the Bible. But John reinterprets that creation story to tell the reader that the Word of God, who was with God in the creation of this world, is now, incredible as it may seem, one of us. That Word "lived among us" and still lives among us.

This creation theme returns in John's Gospel with the scene in the upper room after the resurrection of Jesus, when John twice underscores that these events occur on the "first day of the week," a clear reference to the first of the seven days of creation in Genesis 1. With the resurrection of Jesus, the new creation, the "age to come," has begun. In addition, the risen Jesus breathes on them and says, "Receive the Holy Spirit . . ." (John 20:1, 19, 22). That same "breath" or "wind" or "spirit" brooded over the waters of the first creation.

In these and other ways, John is helping his readers wrap their minds and hearts around the almost unbelievable Good News that God, in the person of this Jewish man from Nazareth, has taken on our human nature and lived among us and died an awful, cruel, demeaning death at our hands for our sake and in our place. That's how much God loves us! And how humble God is!

> What response do you sense in yourself as you ponder all of this? Why don't you tell God how you are feeling and then wait for some kind of response from God.

A reminder: Is it time to take a break from reading and prayer? When you return to the book and to prayer, remember the suggestions for beginning a period of prayer or prayerful reading.

In Paul's letter to the Philippians, we find a wonderful lyric passage that underscores the humility of God. Some Scripture scholars believe that within this text Paul quotes a hymn already well known among the early Christians. Since Paul probably wrote the letter between AD 52 and 62, the hymn might well date back to fifteen to twenty-five years after the death of Jesus.

You might want to read the text out loud if you can do so without disturbing others.

Let the same mind be in you that was in Christ Jesus,

who, though he was in the form of God,
    did not regard equality with God
    as something to be exploited,
but emptied himself,

taking the form of a slave,
being born in human likeness.
And being found in human form,
he humbled himself
and became obedient to the point of death—
even death on a cross.
Therefore God also highly exalted him
and gave him the name
that is above every name,
so that at the name of Jesus
every knee should bend,
in heaven and on earth and under the earth,
and every tongue should confess
that Jesus Christ is Lord,
to the glory of God the Father.
(Philippians 2:5–11)

Ask that these words be burned into your heart and mind so that you will appreciate the humility of God. That's how much God loves us. Again, I encourage you to talk with God as a friend to a friend about all your reactions to this wonderful passage.

To end this section on the humility of God, you may find it helpful to pray the famous hymn by Charles Wesley, "Love Divine, All Loves Excelling." The tune often used is "Hyfrydol," a Welsh tune sung to various hymns. The words speak of the love and humility of God, of the compassion of Jesus, and of the hope that God will finish the work of creation.

Love divine, all loves excelling,
joy of heaven to earth come down,
fix in us thy humble dwelling,
all thy faithful mercies crown.
Jesus, thou art all compassion,
pure, unbounded love thou art;
visit us with thy salvation,
enter every trembling heart.

Breathe, O breathe thy loving Spirit
into every troubled breast;
let us all in thee inherit;
let us find the promised rest.
Take away the love of sinning,
Alpha and Omega be;
end of faith, as its beginning,
set our hearts at liberty.

Come, almighty to deliver,
let us all thy life receive;
suddenly return, and never,
nevermore thy temples leave.
Thee we would be always blessing,
serve thee as thy hosts above,
pray and praise thee without ceasing,
glory in thy perfect love.

Finish then thy new creation,
pure and spotless let us be;
let us see thy great salvation
perfectly restored in thee:
changed from glory into glory,
till in heaven we take our place,
till we cast our crowns before thee,
lost in wonder, love, and praise.

PART 4

LOVING GOD IN JESUS

In the next sessions, I offer suggestions for prayer that might help you grow in love for God through getting to know and love the adult Jesus—first of all, for the kind of human being he was and second, for what God did for us through his death and resurrection. As we begin, remember the suggestions for beginning each period of reading or prayer. Here you might want to ask Jesus to reveal himself to you so that you might know him better, love him more deeply, and be like him. We know another person only when that person reveals him- or herself to us. The same is true for Jesus. So, we ask him to reveal himself to us, and then we let the Gospel stories take hold of our imaginations, trusting that God's Spirit will influence our imaginations to help us know Jesus better.

The Story of Jesus' Life in Mark's Gospel

Sometimes on retreats, I suggest to people who want to know Jesus more intimately that they spend between forty-five minutes and an hour reading the first ten chapters of Mark's Gospel. These ten chapters cover the public life of Jesus up to the last week of his life. The ten chapters can be read without interruption in less than an hour. If you've never done such a thing, you might try it.

If you take this suggestion, remember to ask Jesus to reveal himself to you through this prayerful reading of the Gospel. Then read the ten chapters with care, trusting that Jesus wants to draw you into a closer relationship with him. After you have finished, consider the following questions:

What passages stood out for you? Make a note of them. Then ask yourself what made them stand out. What did you like about Jesus? Was there anything about him that you disliked or that made you afraid of him? You can talk to Jesus about your reactions and see how he responds. You might want to go back to some of the stories that evoked the strongest reactions in you and talk more with Jesus about your reactions.

This exercise may well give you much to discuss with Jesus over a few days. Take as much time as you need or want before moving on. And remember to take a break from praying and reading every so often.

Jesus' Compassion

Next I would like to suggest some passages in the Gospels where the word *compassion* or *pity* is used to describe how Jesus reacts to someone. Here you will recall what we looked at earlier about this word, how compassion almost defines who God is in the Hebrew Bible. As mentioned, the Hebrew word has resonances with the word for womb and so reminds readers of the love a mother has for the child of her womb. When the Old Testament was translated into Greek, the Greek word used had resonances with the word for "gut" and thus speaks of "gut-love." In either case, the word refers to a deeply felt emotion that leads to some action to help the other. These resonances carry over into the New Testament, which was written in Greek. So, when we read in English the words *compassion*, *pity*, and sometimes *mercy*, they have these resonances. Before we take up some passages with these words, remember the suggestions for beginning any session of reading or prayer.

In the very first chapter of Mark we read of Jesus curing a leper. Leprosy was a greatly feared skin disease, and almost from the beginning of the Bible those afflicted by it were banned from the community and required to warn people away if they came near. Touching a leper could give you the disease; touching a leper also made you ritually unclean, unable to participate in worship. If a leper were to become free of the disease in some way, he or she needed to get a seal of approval from a priest before being allowed back into the community. In this passage, therefore, something odd happens right away: the leper is close enough to Jesus to beg him to cleanse him. Jesus must have exuded an aura that made it possible for the man to approach him. Here is the text:

> A leper came to him begging him, and kneeling he said to him, "If you choose, you can make me clean." Moved with pity, Jesus stretched out his hand and touched him, and said to him, "I do choose. Be made clean!" Immediately the leprosy left him, and he was made clean. After sternly warning him he sent him away at once, saying to him, "See that you say nothing to anyone; but go, show yourself to the priest, and offer for your cleansing what Moses commanded, as a testimony to them." But he went out and began to proclaim it freely, and to spread the word,

so that Jesus could no longer go into a town openly, but stayed out in the country; and people came to him from every quarter. (Mark 1:40–45)

Years ago, I read a translation of the leper's words and Jesus' response that has stayed with me. The leper says, "If you want to, you can make me clean," to which Jesus responds, "Of course, I want to; be clean" as he reaches out to touch the man. Clearly that translation touched a chord in me; how about you? Did you notice the phrase "Moved with pity"? The Greek word translated "pity" is the word for gut-love just mentioned. Jesus is reacting as Yahweh reacts to people in deep trouble in the Old Testament. For all Jesus knew, by touching the leper he was taking the risk of getting the disease. At the least, he knew that he would be considered unclean himself for having touched the leper. But still he does it. This scene can be taken as a metaphor for God's compassionate action in becoming a human being among us sinful and wayward human beings. God, in Jesus, takes the risk of becoming tainted by becoming one of us; that's how much God loves us.

Were you able to get an imaginative sense of this scene? How did you react to it? Did you like the way Jesus acted with the man? Have you ever experienced such compassion from

Jesus? Would you want to? Are you attracted to Jesus in this interaction? Do you want to talk with him about your reactions? If so, go ahead.

Did you wonder why Jesus sternly warned the former leper not to talk about his cure? It's hard to know what was on his mind, but it's possible that Jesus did not want people to speak openly about his being the Messiah because of the distorted notions prevalent at that time of what the Messiah would be like. It seems that at this period of Israel's history, expectations of the Messiah's imminent appearance were rife. Most of the Pharisee party expected that the Messiah would bring about a successful war against the Romans, thus ushering in "the age to come," the "Messianic or new age," or "the kingdom of God." Jesus, clearly, has a much different idea of how the Messiah should act, an idea more in line with the suffering servant of Second Isaiah. It is possible that Jesus' rebuke of the demons who announced his identity or even of his warning to this former leper was meant to give him time to convince his people of the real nature of the Messiah.

Let me suggest a couple of other passages that speak of the compassion of Jesus. Again, remember the suggestions on how to begin any period of prayer or reading. The first passage is the story of Jesus raising the son of the widow of Nain.

Soon afterwards he went to a town called Nain, and his disciples and a large crowd went with him. As he approached the gate of the town, a man who had died was being carried out. He was his mother's only son, and she was a widow; and with her was a large crowd from the town. When the Lord saw her, he had compassion for her and said to her, "Do not weep." Then he came forward and touched the bier, and the bearers stood still. And he said, "Young man, I say to you, rise!" The dead man sat up and began to speak, and Jesus gave him to his mother. Fear seized all of them; and they glorified God, saying, "A great prophet has risen among us!" and "God has looked favorably on his people!" This word about him spread throughout Judea and all the surrounding country. (Luke 7:11–17)

Can you picture this scene? The group around Jesus, perhaps boisterous and happy as they approach the village of Nain, suddenly grows quiet as they meet the wailing and somber funeral cortege of the son of a widowed mother. What is Jesus like as he looks on her with compassion, touches the bier, and tells her not to weep? How does Jesus look as he tells the young man to rise? How do you feel as you look at and listen to him? What do you want to say to him? Tell him your reactions, feelings, and thoughts.

The next suggestion is Mark 6:30–34. Jesus has sent the twelve apostles two by two on a missionary journey around

Galilee, and they have just returned, no doubt tired but also eager to tell Jesus about what happened on their mission.

> The apostles gathered around Jesus, and told him all that they had done and taught. He said to them, "Come away to a deserted place all by yourselves and rest a while." For many were coming and going, and they had no leisure even to eat. And they went away in the boat to a deserted place by themselves. Now many saw them going and recognized them, and they hurried there on foot from all the towns and arrived ahead of them. As he went ashore, he saw a great crowd; and he had compassion for them, because they were like sheep without a shepherd; and he began to teach them many things. (Mark 6:30–34)

As the story continues, Jesus feeds the whole crowd by multiplying the few loaves and fish they have. If you take this story as it stands in Mark, Jesus wants to have some time away with the disciples so that he and they can rest up and also talk about their experiences of ministry. But it does not happen.

Can you sense the disappointment of the apostles when they see the crowds that have followed them? Perhaps this was Jesus' first reaction. But what takes over in him is compassion, and he begins to tend to their needs "because they were like sheep without a shepherd."

How do you react to Jesus as you see his heart go out to these people? Are you attracted to him? How do you react to his feeding of them? What does it remind you of? Do you want to talk to him about your reactions, thoughts, and feelings? Such a conversation might lead you into a more personal conversation with him and help you to love him more deeply and want to be more like him.

I remind you to take a break when you have spent some time praying over these texts. No sense in getting overtired. When you feel ready, you might want to go on to the next section, in which we will look at how Jesus tries to convey to his listeners something of who God is through speaking in parables and other stories. As you begin this section, recall the suggestions for beginning any session of reading or praying, made earlier in the book.

The Prodigal Son

Chapter 15 of Luke's Gospel begins: "Now all the tax collectors and sinners were coming near to listen to him. And the Pharisees and the scribes were grumbling and saying, 'This fellow welcomes sinners and eats with them.'" This kind of complaint seems to have been a common one thrown at Jesus. It tells us something about Jesus' practice of table fellowship. He wasn't picky about his companions at meals. As you may know, tax collectors were hated by the Jewish people because they were working for the Roman occupiers or for the puppet king Herod Antipas and also because it was believed that they were enriching themselves by skimming off the top, as it were. "Sinners" in the Bible were people who openly flouted their disregard for the Law and even for God; they were not your garden-variety sinners.

Jesus doesn't get into a tit-for-tat argument with his adversaries. Instead, he tells them three stories. The first asks them what they would do if they owned a hundred sheep and lost one. Essentially, he asks, "Wouldn't you go searching for that lost sheep and then rejoice with friends when you had found it?" The second asks them to consider a woman who loses one of her ten silver coins: "Wouldn't she search all over her house until she finds it and then throw a party for her friends to celebrate her joy?" In these two stories God is compared to that shepherd and that woman; God rejoices more over one sinner who repents than over ninety-nine righteous who need no repentance. In other words, by eating with tax collectors and sinners, Jesus is simply acting the way God acts. Don't you find Jesus and his Father more endearing as you hear such stories?

The third story is one of the great parables in Luke's Gospel, the story often called "The Prodigal Son" but which could more justly be called "The Loving Father." I invite you to read and pray over this story. You will find it in your Bible in Luke 15:11–32. Before you begin reading and praying, remember to ask Jesus to reveal himself to you so that you may love him more and desire more to be his disciple. When you have finished your prayerful contemplation of this parable to your own satisfaction, take a look at the following paragraphs that might help you to deepen your contemplation and prayer.

Jesus' original audience would have been shocked right away by the younger son's request of his father. In effect, he is saying, "I wish you were dead," because that was when he would ordinarily get his inheritance. The original audience would have expected the father to strike his son, perhaps even banish him or order him killed. When they heard that the father agreed to give the son what he wanted, they would have been shocked.

As the story unfolds, it gets worse for the father. The original audience would have felt that the father suffered great embarrassment as word came back about the young son's escapades and finally that he was reduced to working with pigs for a Gentile. (No Jew would keep pigs.) As they heard Jesus tell the story of the young man's decision to come back home, they would have expected that the father would kill his son or, at least, beat him and send him away. Instead they heard Jesus say, "But while he was still far off, his father saw him and was filled with compassion; he ran and put his arms around him and kissed him" (Luke 15:20). Did you notice the word *compassion* here? This father reacted as would Jesus' Abba, his dear Father.

Then the father ordered his servants to dress his son in the best robe and prepare a big party to welcome him home. The audience would have been stunned. Of course, for Jesus this Father is Yahweh, whom Jesus calls Abba (dear Father, or even Dad).

> How do you react to this parable and to the God whom Jesus depicts? Do you sense a greater trust and love for God? Do you feel warmer toward God? Could you call God "Dad?" Do you want to tell God your reactions to this story?

I hope you also noticed how the father treats the older son who became so angry that he, too, insulted his father and would not acknowledge that the prodigal was his brother. "Your son." Remember that this parable was told to the Pharisees and scribes who had attacked Jesus' choice of table companions. With the add-on of the older brother, Jesus was probably talking directly to them. In spite of what we might expect, the older brother was not beaten or berated. Rather, the father said, "Son, you are always with me, and all that is mine is yours. But we had to celebrate and rejoice, because this brother of yours was dead and has come to life; he was lost and has been found" (Luke 15:31).

How do you react to this way of treating enemies? Perhaps this section of the parable, too, will give you something to discuss with Jesus or with his Abba.

Take a break before going to the last session of this section. And when you are ready to begin that section, remember the suggestions for beginning every period of reading or praying.

The Crucifixion

"For God so loved the world that he gave his only Son, so that everyone who believes in him may not perish but may have eternal life" (John 3:16). This verse, arguably the most quoted verse of the New Testament, perhaps of the whole Bible, serves as a segue to this session in which I will offer some thoughts and texts that might help you get to know Jesus better as the one whose life ended in the terrible torture that was crucifixion. Remember the suggestions for beginning any prayer session and that we are asking Jesus to reveal himself so that we can love him more and follow him more closely.

Given some of the images of Jesus common today, a reasonable person might wonder why he was so hated and then killed in this barbaric manner. We have become used to hearing of the caring, gentle shepherd carrying the lamb, the healer of the sick, the comforter of the afflicted. Why would such a man evoke anger, let alone hatred? Yet the Gospels indicate that, almost from the beginning of his public ministry, Jesus was the object of intense anger and even hatred. His life ended with his crucifixion, a thoroughly demeaning and terribly painful way to die.

Executions nowadays are not public spectacles, and so we have little sense of the horror of any execution, let alone crucifixion. That was a very public way for the Romans to show a conquered people who was boss and what would happen to anyone who tried to stand in their way. The man who was crucified was stripped naked, deprived of all dignity as a human being, treated as a slave or worse, forced to die a long, drawn-out, suffocating death as a public spectacle. The Romans made sure that no one for miles around missed what was happening, staging the execution on a hill that commanded a wide view.

It could take days for a crucified man to die an agonizing death, struggling for breath as his arms and legs got weaker and could not lift his body enough to allow him to breathe. This was a way of dying designed to make the condemned person less than human. Remember the words of Second Isaiah describing the suffering servant, words used in the Good Friday liturgy:

Just as there were many who were astonished at him
   —so marred was his appearance, beyond human
      semblance,
   and his form beyond that of mortals. (Isaiah 52:14)
He had no form or majesty that we should look
      at him,
   nothing in his appearance that we should
      desire him.
He was despised and rejected by others;
   a man of suffering and acquainted with infirmity;
and as one from whom others hide their faces
   he was despised, and we held him of no account.
(Isaiah 53:2–3)

> How do you react to these paragraphs? Do you have a sense of the horror of crucifixion? Perhaps you have wondered why Jesus had to die in this way. Let's ponder this question in a prayerful way together.

Why did Jesus die in such a horrible way? It's clear from the Gospels that he made powerful enemies, but we can and do still wonder why they wanted him to die in this way. There must be more to it than that. On the road to Emmaus after his resurrection, Jesus asks the two sad and hopeless disciples, "Was it not necessary that the Messiah should suffer these things and then enter into his glory?" (Luke 24:26). The Crucifixion had to be, Jesus says. Why?

You will recall that the biblical story of creation notes it was "very good" as it came from the creative hand of God and that evil entered through the temptation of Adam and Eve by the serpent, who represented Satan, or as Saint Ignatius put it, the "enemy of human nature." This story is told to indicate that the good in this world has a very powerful enemy indeed. The whole Bible tells the story of how God and this enemy struggle for the hearts and minds of humans. Well, we might say that God threw the final challenge to Satan by becoming one of us, and that must have driven Satan to try everything to overpower God's dream. You might say that Satan thought, *If I can get these humans to kill the Son of God in this inhuman way, that will win the battle.* I know that this is figurative language, but the mystery of evil and the even deeper mystery of Love itself can only be hinted at through story.

It seems that the human predicament was such that only an intervention by God in this totally unexpected and even scandalous way could save us. All human beings, Jew and Gentile alike, were in the same boat. St. Paul makes this point strongly in his letter to the Romans:

We have already charged that all, both Jews and Greeks, are under the power of sin, as it is written:

> "There is no one who is righteous, not even one;
>   there is no one who has understanding,
>   there is no one who seeks God.
> All have turned aside, together they have become
>   worthless;
>   there is no one who shows kindness,
>   there is not even one." (Romans 3:9–12)

A short few verses later he reiterates this assessment: "There is no distinction, since all have sinned and fall short of the glory of God" (Romans 3:22–23).

Moreover, there was and is nothing we human beings can do to escape our predicament. We are like addicts, powerless over our tendency not to be the images of God we are created to be. We have all fallen under the power of Satan and so are condemned to death. We have handed ourselves over to a power beyond our best intentions and resources to contain, and we are doomed to live in fear and trembling all the days of our lives. Jesus calls this power *Satan*; all of us are under his tyranny. Ignatius calls this power "the enemy of human nature," and rightly so, because this power does everything it can to keep us from living as the images of God we are created to be.

God, in his love for us, his wayward children, decides to do something decisive to defeat this enemy, but the cost to God is dreadful. In the person of Jesus of Nazareth, the Son of God, God takes on all that this enemy can do, without ever succumbing to the use of the tactics of the enemy. Jesus never resorts to violence or hatred. He can do nothing else, because God is love. The only alternative I can see to what God did do in Jesus would be to have given up on the whole project of creation. But that also seems out of the question because God is God.

God decides to become a human being, Jesus of Nazareth. We need to take very seriously that Jesus is a human being like us in everything except sin. Jesus must come to a human understanding of who God is and what God has determined to do to save humankind.

How do you react to these last few paragraphs? If you have ever felt that everything seems to be going downhill in our world, then you have some sense of the predicament I just wrote about. If at such times you have felt almost hopeless, then you know how difficult belief in God can be. Perhaps you, too, like me, feel the urge to pray, "I believe; help my unbelief." The crucifixion and resurrection of Jesus are God's answer to the human predicament. We all need to ask God's help to believe this very-difficult-to-believe truth.

Jesus' Human Understanding

Jesus, the human being, comes to an understanding of himself as the Messiah promised by God as the Savior of Israel but a Messiah who runs counter to almost everything the people of Israel expect the Messiah to be. For them, or most of them, the Messiah will be a conquering hero leading Israel to a great military victory over all their enemies and thus ushering in the kingdom of God. After all, he will be God's representative, and God is anything but a loser. (Mind you, two thousand years later, deep in our beings, we still harbor the same ideas about God and winning that the Israelites had.) However, Jesus concludes that God's ways really are not our ways, that the Messiah will win the battle by losing it. He will die a thoroughly degrading, cruel, and painful death on a Roman cross, even forgiving those who crucify him, trusting that this is God's way of saving us human beings from our predicament, a predicament we ourselves have precipitated by not living as human beings created in God's image, designed to help God develop this majestic world.

If you have imagined how difficult it was for Jesus to come to this conclusion about a suffering Messiah, then you may have a sense of why he gets so angry with Peter after his first prediction of the Passion in Mark's Gospel: "Peter took him aside and began to rebuke him. But turning and looking at his disciples, he rebukes Peter and says, 'Get behind me, Satan! For you are setting your mind not on divine things but on human things'" (Mark 8:32–33). Jesus, it seems to me, has come to his conclusion through much agony and prayer, and now Peter tries to turn him aside from that hard-won conviction, thus acting as Satan did when he tempted Jesus in the desert. Jesus is in no mood for that. Perhaps some of the same difficult internal wrestling caused Jesus' agony in the Garden of Gethsemane the night before his death.

How do you react to these paragraphs? Do you want to say anything to Jesus or to God the Father?

The Passion According to Mark

With the background provided in this session so far, you might now read and prayerfully reflect on the Passion narrative in Mark's Gospel. Go to Mark chapters 14 and 15 and read about this great act of God's love for us sinners. Remember the suggestions for beginning any period of prayer. Perhaps the following paragraph will help your reading and prayer.

Jesus is a human being like you, with the same kind of nervous system and body reactions as you have. Don't let thoughts of his divinity throw you off these human reactions. We don't know anything about what it's like to be God, but we do know what it's like to be a human being. In fact, *the best way for us to know God is to contemplate Jesus as a human being, and especially Jesus on the cross*. What you are contemplating is God's full revelation of who he is in Jesus, a human being like us. You can use your imagination to sense his reactions. Trust that he will reveal himself to you. Talk to him about your reactions and feelings and whatever else you want to say to him. When you are finished, you might want to write something about this period of prayer in your journal. Then you might want to take a break.

Remember the suggestions for beginning any prayer session. Perhaps it will help you reflect on the greatest act of God's love for us by prayerfully reading the following summary by the Episcopal priest and preacher Fleming Rutledge in *The Crucifixion: Understanding the Death of Jesus Christ*.

At the historical time and place of his inhuman and god-less crucifixion, all the demonic Powers loose in the world convened in Jerusalem and unleashed their forces upon the incarnate Son of God. Derelict, outcast, and godfor-saken, he hung there as the representative of all humanity, and suffered condemnation in place of all humanity, to break the Power of Sin and Death over all humanity.

None of this would avail against the world's evil were it not for the righteousness of God. . . . The power of God to make right what has been wrong is what we see, by faith, in the resurrection of Jesus Christ on the third day. Unless God is the one who raises the dead and calls into existence the things that do not exist, there cannot be serious talk of forgiveness for the worst of the worst—the mass murders, tortures, and serial killings—or even for the least of the worst—the quotidian offenses against our common humanity that cause marriages to fail, friendships to end, enterprises to collapse, and silent misery to be the common lot of millions. "All for sin could not atone; thou must save, and thou alone." This is what is happening on Golgotha. All the manifold biblical images with their richness, complexity, and depth come together as one to say this: the righteousness of God is revealed in the cross of Christ. . . . From within "Adam's" (our) human flesh, the incarnate Son fought with and was victorious over Satan—on our behalf and in our place. Only this power, this transcendent victory won by the Son of God, is capable of reorienting the *kosmos* [the universe] to its rightful Creator. This is what the righteousness of God has achieved through the cross and resurrection, is now accomplishing by the power of the Spirit, and will complete in the day of Christ Jesus. (610–611)

I realize that these lines are a lot to take in, but they will repay your prayerful consideration. Rutledge wrote her long, scholarly book because she believes that the Christian churches have avoided preaching effectively on the Crucifixion and have thus failed to preach the full powerful message of the gospel to the people of God. I agree with her.

How did you react to Rutledge's words? Did they puzzle you? If so, you can ask God to help you understand more deeply the mystery of the crucifixion and resurrection of Jesus. If what she wrote made sense to you, what do you want to say to God? Tell God and then see how the conversation develops.

Jesus Died for the Ungodly as Well as the Godly

When you are ready, some further reflections might help you grow in love for God. (Remember the suggestions for beginning any period of prayer or reading.) One of the hardest truths about God for many of us to stomach (and, therefore, even to want to imitate) is that Jesus died for the ungodly as well as the godly. All of us, I believe, harbor a conviction that there are some people who really are so bad that they deserve God's condemnation and so can never be forgiven. This conviction helps us live more easily with our own shame at what we have done or thought and our own lack of self-esteem: "At least I'm not as bad as . . ."

I can attest to having such feelings. One of the ways I kept myself from facing my own alcoholism was by comparing myself with "them," those real drunks who were alcoholics. I was not like them. Of course, I could and did say, "There but for the grace of God go I," but in my heart I didn't believe it. I was not like "them." I was not powerless. Of course, I had to avoid looking at the full reality of my drinking to keep up this delusion. I have also used a similar argument to console myself when I become aware of my other sins. I'm not *that* bad. But Paul is insistent: "All have sinned and fall short of the glory of God" (Romans 3:23).

This means that Jesus died for everyone, including the worst sinners we can think of, including, for example, Judas Iscariot. And thank God that this is true. Each one of us knows that there are dark places within us that make us capable of great evil. Why are horror movies and novels so popular? Haven't you reveled in the horrible deaths those "evil monsters" suffer on television, in movies, and in novels? An honest look at ourselves reveals aspects that we hope will never see the light of day. Jesus died for those parts of us as well as for the serial killers and rapists of our world. If we let this sink in, I believe, we will be freed from fear. Then we will know in our guts the truth of those words of the first letter of St. John: "There is no fear in love, but perfect love casts out fear; for fear has to do with punishment, and whoever fears has not reached perfection in love. We love because he first loved us" (1 John 4:18–19).

In becoming human in Jesus and dying in such a degrading and shameful way, God has done the humanly unimaginable and unthinkable for love of us humans, all of whom have chosen in big and little ways to be inhuman. And make no mistake, if God were to become human again, we humans would kill him again, as Dostoyevsky makes clear in the Grand Inquisitor parable told in *The Brothers Karamazov*. Truly "God so loved the world that he gave his only Son, so that everyone who believes in him may not perish but may have eternal life" (John 3:16).

How did you react to these few paragraphs? Did you think of people you could not forgive? Are there some people you are sure are in hell? You can talk over with Jesus all your reactions and questions. You may want to ask to have the same mind and heart and bodily reactions as Jesus. And if you can't ask for that, you can tell Jesus you can't and see where the conversation goes. Just remember that God relishes your honesty with him, an indication of your trust in his love for you.

As we end this session on Jesus' crucifixion, you might be helped to express your love for God and your gratitude for God's great love for you and for all of us by prayerfully reading the ending of Fleming Rutledge's great work.

> Several times in this book the reader has encountered an intimately personal testimony by the apostle Paul in his letter to the church in Galatia. For writer and readers alike, these words can be our heart's comfort and joy, for now and for all the days to come, whatever befalls: "I have been crucified with Christ; it is no longer I who live, but Christ who lives in me; and the life I now live in the flesh I live by faith in the Son of God, who loved me and gave himself for me" (Galatians 2:20).

The author of this volume concludes by making this confession together with Christopher Smart (an eighteenth-century English poet):

> Awake, arise, lift up your voice,
> let Easter music swell;
> rejoice in Christ, again rejoice
> and on his praises dwell.

> Oh, with what gladness and surprise
> the saints their Savior greet;
> nor will they trust their ears and eyes

but by his hands and feet,
those hands of liberal love indeed
in infinite degree,
those feet still free to move and bleed
for millions,
and for me.
Amen.
(Rutledge cites a hymn by Christopher Smart, with
the final five words separated and italicized for
emphasis.)

PART 5

"A CONTEMPLATION FOR ATTAINING LOVE FOR GOD"

There are four points of the Contemplation for Attaining Love. The exercise itself is the very last one proposed by Ignatius of Loyola in his *Spiritual Exercises*. Ignatius hopes that this contemplation would help us attain not God's love for us but our love for God. God's love for us is a given; it does not depend on anything we are or do. I know that this is a hard lesson to learn; I'm still asking God for help to take it in. I hope it's sinking in to you as well. This contemplation is suggested as a way for us to fall more deeply in love with God.

Ignatius makes two comments before he gets to the Contemplation. I mentioned these two prenotes in an earlier section. The first is that love ought to show itself "in deeds more than in words," but the second makes a profound point: "love consists in mutual communication" (*Sp. Ex.* 230). Here he insists that God wants something from us: our acceptance of his love and our love in return. Think about that. God, who needs nothing, wants our freely given love. God loves us that much; it means something to God that we love in return.

Next, Ignatius proposes points that may help us respond to God with mutual love. Ignatius asks us to contemplate ourselves and our world in such a way that we will become passionately attracted to God—so that we will realize that we are immersed in God's love and be drawn to love God in return.

As we begin, let's remember that we are in the presence of God right now and throughout the day. God is looking at us with love and hopes that we will return the love. Ignatius suggests that we then ask for what we want: "Here it will be to ask for interior knowledge of all the good I have received, so that acknowledging this with gratitude, I may be able to love and serve his Divine Majesty in everything" (*Sp. Ex.* 233). In effect, Ignatius suggests that we ask to love God "with all your heart, and with all your soul, and with all your mind, and with all your strength" (Mark 12:30).

Ignatius calls this a *contemplation*, not a meditation. It is like the contemplations of the Gospels. In those, we allow the story to capture our imagination so that the story becomes *our* story, a story in which we have a part to play. When the magic works, we become part of the story of Jesus in which he reveals himself to us and we to him. So, too, in this contemplation, it is not a question of thinking about the points but of asking to experience the world as it truly is. When we are caught up in the flow of this contemplation, we become contemplatives in action—that is, we become more and more aware of being in a world "charged with the grandeur of God," as Gerard Manley Hopkins put it in his poem "God's Grandeur." We become "the beholder" that is wanted, as the same poet writes in "Hurrahing in Harvest." Moreover, we fall in love with God, who has done all these marvels.

The First Point: Practice Remembering

Ignatius puts it this way:

> This is to bring to memory the benefits received—creation, redemption, and particular gifts—pondering with great affection how much God Our Lord has done for me, how much He has given me of what He has, and further, how according to His divine plan, it is the Lord's wish, as far as He is able, to give me Himself. Then I shall reflect within myself and consider what, in all reason and justice, I ought for my part to offer and give to His Divine Majesty, that is to say, all I possess and myself as well, saying, as one making a gift with great love:
>
> "Take, Lord, and receive all my liberty, my memory, my understanding, and my entire will, all that I have and possess. You gave it all to me; to you I give it all back. All is yours, dispose of it entirely according to your will. Give

me the grace to love you, for that is enough for me." (*Sp. Ex.* 234)

With God's help, recall all the gifts you have been given throughout your life. Think of this review as a way to retrieve some of your history with God. The Israelites often did this sort of thing, and we have psalms that indicate such prayer, for example, Psalm 104 or 136. In them the Israelites recalled the great deeds of God. As you begin your own prayer, you may be encouraged by this statement of Frederick Buechner near the beginning of his first memoir, *The Sacred Journey*. Now a Presbyterian minister, he is about to begin talking about his early life when he hardly thought of God.

> What quickens my pulse now is the stretch ahead rather than the one behind, and it is mainly for some clue to where I am going that I search through where I have been, for some hint as to who I am becoming or failing to become that I delve into what used to be. I listen back to a time when nothing was much farther from my thoughts than God for an echo of the gutturals and sibilants and vowellessness by which I believe that even then God was addressing me out of my life as he addresses us all. And it is because I believe that, that I think of my life and of the lives of everyone who has ever lived, or will ever live, as not just journeys through time but as sacred journeys. (6)

Do you dare think of your life as a sacred journey? Well, along with Buechner, I believe your life, and everyone else's, is exactly that. I am suggesting that you engage in this period of prayer to get a sense of that sacredness and also, in keeping with the nature of this book, to grow in love for God.

You could begin with a memory of your childhood or some recent memory of a gift and then let the memories rise spontaneously. Some people have spent one period of prayer on each of the different seasons of life, letting the memories arise, trusting the Spirit of God to inspire their memories. You may want to do the same.

Sometimes people are helped by reading Psalm 139 slowly and prayerfully, letting that psalm awaken memories. After you finish to your satisfaction, letting the memories of your life arise as God's gift to you, you might use the refrain of Psalm 136. That psalm rehearses in God's presence the whole salvation history of the Israelites line by line; each memory is followed by the refrain, "for his steadfast love endures forever." Here are a few lines to get you started.

> "O give thanks to the LORD, for he is good,
>   for his steadfast love endures forever. . . .
> Who alone does great wonders,
>   for his steadfast love endures forever;
> who by understanding made the heavens,

> for his steadfast love endures forever."
> (Psalm 136:1, 4–5)
>
> Create your own verses, such as "Who placed me in my family and filled my life with people / for his steadfast love endures forever / who awakened in me certain gifts when I was still a child, gifts that have enriched my life / for his steadfast love endures forever." As you recall each of God's gifts to you, repeat "for his steadfast love endures forever" after each one.
>
> As a final prayer to end this point, see if you want to say—and if you can mean—the prayer Ignatius puts at the end of the point: "Take, Lord, and receive. . . ." I have to admit that I want to be able to say this prayer with my whole heart and soul but am still not there. So, I often beg God to help me love and trust him this much. I think of this prayer as one I will be praying until I die, asking that I may so love God.

I am emboldened to think along these lines by a story told by N. T. Wright in *Paul and the Faithfulness of God* (619–620), who writes about Rabbi Akiba, a famous rabbi who lived a century after Jesus. Akiba had backed a messiah who tried to overthrow Roman rule, and he was now being tortured to death by the Romans. His disciples were surprised to hear him reciting the *Shema* (the first commandment) over and over as he was dying. They asked why he was doing this. He replied that he had always wanted to love God with his whole *nephesh*, his whole soul or being. All his life he had been troubled by the meaning of that part of the *Shema* and now he had a chance to live it out. That's going the extra mile, isn't it? But it does bring out the difficulty of loving God with all one's heart, soul, mind, and strength. We may not be tested as was the rabbi, but we can all agree with him that we need God's help to love God. Just as we need to pray all our lives, "I believe, help my unbelief," so we need to pray, "I love you, help my unlove" all the days of our lives.

Before you go on to the second point, you might want to take a break, as also before the third and fourth points. When you are ready to go on with the book and your prayer, you can take up the second point, remembering the suggestions about beginning every time of prayer.

The Second Point: Notice Divine Presence and Love

Ignatius's second point reads this way:

> To see how God dwells in creatures—in the elements, giving being, in the plants, causing growth, in the animals, producing sensation, and in humankind, granting the gift of understanding—and so how He dwells also in me, giving me being, life and sensation, and causing me to understand. To see too how He makes a temple of me, as I have been created in the likeness and image of His Divine Majesty. Again, to reflect within myself in the way indicated in Point 1, or in some other way I find better. The same procedure is to be followed in each of the following points. (*Sp. Ex.* 235)

Remember what we reflected on earlier, about the love of God beating at the heart of the universe. This point may help to increase your sense of how deeply God is embedded in this vast universe. Often our imagination of creation is limited to a sense of God having created everything in the distant past. This point may help our imaginations soar to previously unimagined heights and then sink to previously unimagined depths.

God dwells in galaxies we don't even know exist as well as in our own. God dwells in stars and planets, and in slugs and mosquitoes, and in microbes; God dwells in red roses and cardinals and in smelly seaweed and cawing crows. God lives in your dearest friend and in your worst enemy. And God dwells in me and you. Let your imagination go. That's what this whole contemplation is about. When you think you have gone as far as you can, make sure you tell God how you are feeling about God before you end. Are you experiencing a deeper love for God? Are you able to say and mean a bit more the prayer after the first point?

When you're ready, you can go on to the third point, remembering the suggestions for beginning prayer.

The Third Point: Imagine What God Creates Right Now

The third point goes,

> To consider how God works and labors on my behalf in all created things on the face of the earth, i.e., "He behaves in the same way as a person at work," as in the heavens, elements, plants, fruits, cattle, etc. He gives being, conserves life, grants growth and feeling, etc. Then to reflect within myself. (*Sp. Ex.* 236)

This is rather amazing, isn't it? God is likened to a servant or a slave who enjoys working for us in everything that exists. Because of the marvels of modern scientific discoveries, we have some sense of how interrelated everything in the universe is.

Here we are asked to imagine how God is working to hold everything together in harmony. God's creative work is never done. Again, let your imagination go wherever it takes you, to the farthest star in our universe and to the smallest microscopic element within us. God is holding everything together with love; God's loving heart throbs at the heart of everything. Psalm 8 might help you to develop your conversation with God at this point.

> O LORD, our Sovereign,
>> how majestic is your name in all the earth!
> You have set your glory above the heavens.
>> Out of the mouths of babes and infants
> you have founded a bulwark because of your foes,
>> to silence the enemy and the avenger.
> When I look at your heavens, the work of your
>>> fingers,
>> the moon and the stars that you have established;
> what are human beings that you are mindful
>>> of them,
>> mortals that you care for them?
> Yet you have made them a little lower than God,
>> and crowned them with glory and honor.
> You have given them dominion over the works of
>>> your hands;
>> you have put all things under their feet,
> all sheep and oxen,

> and also the beasts of the field,
> the birds of the air, and the fish of the sea,
>   whatever passes along the paths of the seas.
> O LORD, our Sovereign,
>   how majestic is your name in all the earth!
>
> Tell God how you are feeling now. Can you more honestly say and mean the prayer at the end of the first point?

When you are ready, you can take up the fourth point, remembering to begin with the suggestions for beginning every period of prayer.

The Fourth Point: Take Stock of Your Gifts

The fourth point reads,

> To see how all that is good and every gift descends from on high; so, my limited power descends from the supreme and infinite power above, and similarly justice, goodness, pity, mercy, etc., as rays descend from the sun, and waters from a fountain. Then to finish reflecting within myself, as has been said. (*Sp. Ex.* 237)

Here, I believe, Ignatius is recalling what happened to him as he neared the end of his months of prayer and reflection in Manresa. In his "Reminiscences" (see Ignatius of Loyola, *Personal Writings*, 26) he tells of an experience he had one day at Mass: "As the body of the Lord was being raised, he saw with his interior eyes some things like white rays which were coming from above." He notes that he cannot explain this, but he was convinced that he had seen how Jesus was present in the Eucharist. With this point we are asking for a great grace from God: to be able to sense God's presence in everything that exists.

I can recall only one time when something vaguely like this happened to me. I was leading a group of African Jesuit scholastics in their annual three-day retreat just before Christmas at a retreat house on the outskirts of Nairobi, Kenya. Each evening we had a holy hour in the chapel before the Blessed Sacrament, which was contained in a large monstrance. The monstrance was made to resemble rays of the sun around the host. One evening as I prayed with the group, I felt that I was praying before the center of the world, that all the energy of the world was coming from that center, Jesus in our midst.

Can you recall a time or place when you just felt overcome with warmth and joy and a desire to stay in that place forever? A time when you felt just right about everything around you and wanted something but could not name what it was? Gerard Manley Hopkins must have felt something like that and then composed the poem "God's Grandeur" in which he tried to express the wonder of that moment or those moments.

A reminder: Take a break if you have been reading and praying for some time. When you return, we will take a look at the Song of Solomon, or Song of Songs, as a help to grow in love with God.

The Song of Solomon: Celebrating Intense, Personal Love

Both Jews and Christians have wondered why the Song of Solomon is in the Bible. After all, it seems to be a collection of love poems between a woman and a man who celebrate their love in strongly erotic, sexual language. In my Jesuit novitiate sixty-seven years ago, we were not allowed to read the book because of its erotic language. Yet both Jewish and Christian traditions have seen in this book of love poems a celebration of the love between God and humans; hence, it is a beloved book of the Bible. I want to give you a taste of some of these poems as a help to appreciate how much God loves you and to inspire further your own love for God. As with all my suggestions, if they help, use them; if not, skip them. As you begin this section, remember the suggestions for beginning every period of prayer or reading.

Chapter 2 of the Song has the following section in which the voices of both the bride and the bridegroom are heard. See if these voices touch your heart.

> The voice of my beloved!
>   Look, he comes,
> leaping upon the mountains,
>   bounding over the hills.
> My beloved is like a gazelle
>   or a young stag.
> Look, there he stands
>   behind our wall,
> gazing in at the windows,
>   looking through the lattice.
> My beloved speaks and says to me:
> "Arise, my love, my fair one,
>   and come away;
> for now the winter is past,
>   the rain is over and gone.
> The flowers appear on the earth;
>   the time of singing has come,
> and the voice of the turtledove
>   is heard in our land.
> The fig tree puts forth its figs,

and the vines are in blossom;
they give forth fragrance.
Arise, my love, my fair one,
    and come away.
O my dove, in the clefts of the rock,
    in the covert of the cliff,
let me see your face,
    let me hear your voice;
for your voice is sweet,
    and your face is lovely. . . ."
My beloved is mine and I am his;
    he pastures his flock among the lilies.
Until the day breathes
    and the shadows flee,
turn, my beloved, be like a gazelle
    or a young stag on the cleft mountains.
(Song of Solomon 2:8–17)

In the opening lines we hear the voice of the bride speaking of the bridegroom, using terms of endearment, likening him to a young stag leaping toward her and then peering into her window. Then the bridegroom speaks tender words of invitation, calling her to come away with him now that winter is over and spring is upon them. He uses descriptive words that indicate how lovely he finds her.

> Think of God as speaking so tenderly and passionately to you, telling you how much he is attracted to you. How do you react? Be sure to tell God what you are feeling and thinking.

At the end, the bride speaks again, telling anyone who will listen how attractive she finds the bridegroom: "My beloved is mine, and I am his," a phrase that is repeated in slightly different form in chapter 6: "I am my beloved's and my beloved is mine; he pastures his flock among the lilies." Johann Sebastian Bach uses these lines in a section of his cantata *Wachet Auf*, "Wake Up," but he changes "beloved" to "friend" and makes it into a duet. In German, the bride sings *"Mein Freund ist mein,"* "My friend is mine," to which the bridegroom (Christ) replies, *"Und ich bin dein,"* "And I am yours." Then their voices blend into one as they continue to sing to and with one another.

> As you let this passage resonate in your heart, you might want to say to Jesus, "My friend is mine," and then see if you hear Jesus saying "And I am yours."

In chapter 4, the bridegroom speaks with great affection of the beauty of the bride he loves. He begins with these words: "How beautiful you are, my love, how very beautiful" (Song of Solomon 4:1) and then goes on to describe her beauty. Some of his words might make you smile or laugh, because he uses images from his farm and his orchard. Then he says,

> You have ravished my heart, my sister, my bride,
> you have ravished my heart with a glance of
> your eyes,
> with one jewel of your necklace.
> How sweet is your love, my sister, my bride!
> how much better is your love than wine,
> and the fragrance of your oils than any spice!
> (Song of Solomon 4:9–10)

Remember that these verses are in the Bible because both Jews and Christians believe that this poetry expresses God's love for us and our love for God. The biblical writer is using the love between a man and a woman to convey something about God's love for us and our love for God.

Can you imagine God saying something like these words to you? If so, let God know of your reactions.

The bride expresses her admiration of and attraction to her beloved in chapter 5 in these words:

> My beloved all radiant and ruddy,
> distinguished among ten thousand.

His head is the finest gold;
    his locks are wavy,
    black as a raven. (Song of Solomon 5:10–11)

She then goes on to describe him in great detail and with varied images and ends thus:

His speech is most sweet,
    and he is altogether desirable.
This is my beloved and this is my friend,
O daughters of Jerusalem. (Song of Solomon 5:16)

Over the centuries both men and women have found that the Song of Solomon describes their relationship with God. Perhaps you, too, will find it descriptive of your own relationship with God—or perhaps you will realize that you want such a relationship with God.

A reminder: You might need a break from reading and prayer. When you are ready, the following excerpts from Augustine's Confessions may help you to grow in love with God.

Augustine's Confessions:
Our God-Shaped Longing

In the opening lines of *Confessions*, St. Augustine reflects on the majesty of God the Creator and his own insignificance as he begins to write about his life. These lines may supplement the Contemplation that Ignatius suggests. Here are excerpts from the beginning of the First Book of *Confessions*. The words in italics here and in the following are citations from Scripture.

> *Can any praise be worthy of the Lord's majesty? How magnificent his strength! How inscrutable his wisdom!* Man is one of your creatures, Lord, and his instinct is to praise you. He bears about him the mark of death, the sign of his own sin, to remind him that you *thwart the proud.* But still, since he is a part of your creation, he wishes to praise you. The thought of you stirs him so deeply that he cannot be content unless he praises you, because you made us

for yourself and our hearts find no peace until they rest in you. (21)

The last lines may be the most quoted of *Confessions*. Those of us who acknowledge our desire for God and want to love and praise God are in good company: the whole of the human race. In various autobiographies and novels, I have found instances of the sudden eruption of a feeling of great well-being, accompanied by a desire to express thanks or praise. Sometimes the one who experiences this eruption is an unbeliever and doesn't know whom to praise or thank. The mystery novelist P. D. James, herself a believer, must know of this experience. In at least two of her novels, she describes such experiences in characters who do not have religious faith. For example, in *Original Sin*, one of her detective stories featuring Chief Inspector Adam Dalgliesh, James writes of his Scotland Yard subordinate Kate Mishkin:

Standing now between the glitter of the water and the high, delicate blue of the sky, she felt an extraordinary impulse which had visited her before and which she thought must be as close as she could ever get to a religious experience. She was possessed by a need, almost physical in its intensity, to pray, to praise, to say thank you, without knowing to whom, to shout with a joy that was deeper than the joy she felt in her own physical well-being and achievements or even in the beauty of the physical world. (148)

Perhaps such a story will remind you of a similar experience you have had and thus add some energy to your conversation with God.

In the following excerpt, Augustine reflects that his desire for God is a desire that God dwell in him. This thought leads him to pray to God about what this might mean. Perhaps prayerful reflection on the following two paragraphs will remind you of Ignatius's second point in the "Contemplation to Attain the Love of God": to notice divine presence in your life.

How shall I call upon my God for aid, when the call I make is for my Lord and my God to come into myself? What place is there in me to which my God can come, what place that can receive the God who made heaven and earth? Does this then mean, O Lord my God, that there is in me something fit to contain you? Can even heaven and earth, which you made and in which you made me, contain you? Or, since nothing that exists could exist without you, does this mean that whatever exists does, in this sense, contain you? If this is so, since I too exist, why do I ask you to come into me? For I should not be there at all unless, in this way, you were already present within me.

I am not in hell, and yet you are there too, for *if I sink down to the world beneath, you are present still*. So, then, I should be null and void and could not exist at all, if you, my God, were not in me.

Or is it rather that I should not exist, unless I existed in you? For *all things find in you their origin, their impulse, the center of their being*. This, Lord, is the true answer to my question. But if I exist in you, how can I call upon you to come to me? And where would you come from? For you, my God, have said that you *fill heaven and earth*, but I cannot go beyond the bounds of heaven and earth so that you may leave them to come to me. (*Confessions*, 22)

Augustine's dialogue with God about his desire for God to dwell in him leads him deeper and deeper into the real union that God wants with all of us. He realizes that God is already as near to him as his own heart, perhaps nearer. Finally, he ends this section with the following prayer to God:

You, my God, are supreme, utmost in goodness, mightiest and all-powerful, most merciful and most just. You are the most hidden from us and yet the most present amongst us, the most beautiful and yet the most strong, ever enduring and yet we cannot comprehend you. You are unchangeable and yet you change all things. You are never new, never old, and yet all things have new life from you. . . . You support, you fill, and you protect all things. You create them, nourish them, and bring them to perfection. You seek to make them your own, though you lack for nothing. You love your creatures, but with a gentle love. You treasure them, but without apprehension. . . . You are my God, my Life, my holy Delight, but is this enough to say of you? Can any man say enough when he speaks of you? Yet woe betide those who are silent about you! For even those who are most gifted with speech cannot find words to describe you. (*Confessions*, 23)

How do you react to Augustine's prayer to God? Does he give you some new ways of talking with God or some new things to say to God? Do you sense that you are growing in your own desire for God? Do you feel more ready to say and mean the prayer at the end of the first point of Ignatius's "Contemplation to Attain the Love of God"?

Finally, you might use the words of the hymn "Joyful, Joyful, We Adore Thee" to express your own growing love for God. Henry Van Dyke composed the poem, and you have probably heard or sung it to the tune by Ludwig van Beethoven.

> Joyful, joyful, we adore you,
> God of glory, Lord of love;
> Hearts unfold like flow'rs before you,
> Op'ning to the sun above.
> Melt the clouds of sin and sadness;
> Drive the dark of doubt away;
> Giver of immortal gladness,
> Fill us with the light of day!

All Your works with joy surround You,
Earth and heav'n reflect Your rays,
Stars and angels sing around You,
Center of unbroken praise.
Field and forest, vale and mountain,
Flowr'y meadow, flashing sea,
Chanting bird and flowing fountain
Praising You eternally!

Always giving and forgiving,
Ever blessing, ever blest,
Well-spring of the joy of living,
Ocean-depth of happy rest!
Loving Father, Christ our Brother,
Let Your light upon us shine;
Teach us how to love each other,
Lift us to the joy divine.

Mortals, join the mighty chorus,
Which the morning stars began;
God's own love is reigning o'er us,
Joining people hand in hand.
Ever singing, march we onward,
Victors in the midst of strife;
Joyful music leads us sunward,
In the triumph song of life.

PART 6

LOVE OF NEIGHBOR

Repeatedly in these pages we have noticed God's humble love for us and, in the process, grown in our response, in our love for God. We have also noted that God's love for us has led to our creation in God's image and likeness. We have recognized God's invitation to us to cooperate with God in bringing about the kingdom of God on this earth. We come now to the second great teaching on how to live truly as people made in God's image and how to cooperate with God—namely, that we should love our neighbor as ourselves. In these last few sections, I want to offer you suggestions that may help you to live out this teaching. I will begin by suggesting a contemplation of the opening scene of the Last Supper in the Gospel according to John.

Jesus Washes the Feet of His Disciples

Through his actions primarily, but also through his words, Jesus demonstrates God's humble love. The washing of the disciples' feet in John's Gospel is a prime example of such a demonstration by actions and then in words. The first few verses in the scene of the Last Supper in John 13 are one sentence in Greek—written this way, I'm sure, to make the point that God is servant love. Here is the New Revised Standard Version's translation:

Now before the festival of the Passover, Jesus knew that his hour had come to depart from this world and go to the Father. Having loved his own who were in the world, he loved them to the end. The devil had already put it into the heart of Judas son of Simon Iscariot to betray him. And during supper Jesus, knowing that the Father had given all things into his hands, and that he had come

> from God and was going to God, got up from the table,
> took off his outer robe, and tied a towel around himself.
> Then he poured water into a basin and began to wash the
> disciples' feet and to wipe them with the towel that was
> tied around him. (John 13:1–5)

Clearly, the translators have decided to break the one sentence of the Greek original into multiple sentences. Here are these lines as one sentence: "Now before the festival of the Passover, knowing that his hour had come to depart from this world and go to the Father, having loved his own who were in the world and loving them to the end, the devil having already put it into the heart of Judas Iscariot to betray him, during supper, knowing that the Father had given all things into his hands and that he had come from God and was going to God, Jesus got up from the table, took off his outer robe, tied a towel around himself and poured water into a basin and began to wash the disciples' feet and to wipe them with the towel that was tied around him."

It's an ungainly sentence in English, of course. That's why translators break the sentence into more than one. But the original does indicate what a great act of humility and love for others this was. The sentence emphasizes Jesus' knowledge of himself as the Son of God and also brings out that he washes Judas's feet, knowing that Judas has decided to betray him. The Gospel writer wants readers to gasp with awe at the lengths God is willing to go for us. Jesus shows in action who God is. No wonder Peter is aghast at what Jesus wants to do for him!

> Were you able to imagine the scene? How did you react? Did you notice that Jesus washed Judas's feet? How did that make you feel? Did Jesus wash your feet? If not, would you want him to do so? Questions such as these may help you engage in a conversation with Jesus.

Now we come to Jesus' explanation of what he has done.

> After he had washed their feet, had put on his robe, and had returned to the table, he said to them, "Do you know what I have done to you? You call me Teacher and Lord—and you are right, for that is what I am. So if I, your Lord and Teacher, have washed your feet, you also ought to wash one another's feet. For I have set you an example, that you also should do as I have done to you. Very truly, I tell you, servants are not greater than their master, nor are messengers greater than the one who sent them. If you know these things, you are blessed if you do them." (John 13:12–17)

This last point brings us to the second great commandment: "You shall love your neighbor as yourself." Jesus asks his disciples—and through them, us—to take care of others as he has taken care of them, and us. Their love for Jesus will naturally spill over into wanting to be like him in caring for others.

Spend some time with this scene and in a conversation with Jesus.

For the next few sessions, we shall engage in prayerful exercises and reflections that I hope you will find helpful in your own desire to love your neighbor as yourself.

Jesus' Last Words to the Disciples: Love One Another

Keep in mind that the writer of John's Gospel is describing Jesus' last night on earth. The first passage is from chapter 15. In the beginning of this chapter Jesus speaks of the vine and the branches, comparing himself to the vine and his disciples to the branches. Then he says,

> This is my commandment, that you love one another as I have loved you. No one has greater love than this, to lay down one's life for one's friends. You are my friends if you do what I command you. I do not call you servants any longer, because the servant does not know what the master is doing; but I have called you friends, because I have made known to you everything that I have heard from my Father. You did not choose me but I chose you. And I appointed you to go and bear fruit, fruit that will last, so that the Father will give you whatever you ask him in my

name. I am giving you these commands so that you may love one another. (John 15:12–17)

Imagine the scene. You know, better than the disciples who were there, what will happen the next day. Hence you know that these are some of the last moments Jesus will have with them. Can you feel the atmosphere in that upper room as Jesus speaks from his heart? Let Jesus' words wash over you. Hear them spoken to you as personally as they were spoken to the disciples at the supper. In these last moments of his life he is calling you a friend and asking you to be his friend and to "love one another." How do you react? Do you want to speak to Jesus, to tell him anything? Go ahead and also listen for his reply.

Remember to take a break before you move on.

When Jesus Prayed for Us

In chapter 17 of John's Gospel we read the last words Jesus speaks before he moves into the garden where he will be betrayed. We are listening to him talk to his beloved Father at this awe-filled time.

> I encourage you to read the entire chapter 17 in your Bible or online. Ask Jesus to reveal himself to you, and then read this great prayer slowly, aloud if you find this helpful, pausing whenever you are so moved, especially if you want to say something to Jesus or to the Father. When you are finished reading, what follows may help you with your prayerful response to Jesus.

"This is eternal life, that they may know you, the only true God, and Jesus Christ whom you have sent" (John 17:3). *Know* here means heart knowledge, the kind of knowledge spouses and friends have of one another. This is the knowledge of God that Jesus, with his actions and words, has tried to convey to his people and to all of us throughout his public life. Did you notice how intimate he wants us to be with him and his Father? He wants us to be one with him and with one another as he and the Father are one: "As you, Father, are in me and I am in you, may they also be in us . . . so that they may be one, as we are one, I in them and you in me, that they may become completely one . . . so that the love with which you have loved me may be in them, and I in them" (John 17:21–23, 26).

What was most on Jesus' mind and heart on this night before his horrible death was not what awaited him the following day but rather his disciples in that upper room and all those who would follow them, you and me among them. And what he wanted for us was the same kind of intimacy with God that he has, an intimacy of love that would spill over into all our other relationships.

Allow your mind and heart to absorb this knowledge: that Jesus wanted you and me to be as close to the Father as he was. The unity Jesus prays for is, of course, God's very dream in creating our universe and us human beings in God's image, that we would live in unity with God, with one another, and with the whole universe. Have you ever imagined a world like that? Can you now imagine it? If you can imagine it, how do you react to such a world? You might want to ask Jesus to help you to love others as he loves them. Perhaps you have more to talk about with Jesus.

Beyond Our Human Capacity?

Before we go any further on this topic of love of neighbor, I need to make something as clear as I can. What Jesus prays for and commands—that we love one another—is very often beyond our capability to do by ourselves. As I was working on this section of the book, I had a session of spiritual direction with a very prayerful woman that brought home to me one of the great difficulties of speaking of this commandment of love without triggering sometimes massive feelings of failure and debilitating guilt. I realized that for this woman and for many others, guilt about not being able to love certain people or even a large number of people consumes them and often keeps them from engaging in a personal relationship with God.

Many people feel unworthy of Jesus' friendship because they do not or cannot love certain people. They have confessed this failure to love any number of times but have not changed even though they want to. Some of them, including the woman just mentioned, have had very deep, personal, and consoling conversations with Jesus interrupted by thoughts of their unworthiness that challenge the authenticity of the consoling experiences. When this happens, they stop praying and think of themselves as phonies. In sessions of spiritual direction, I try to help them discern which experiences come from God—the positive experiences of closeness to God or the disturbing experiences of doubt. Each time, it seems to me, we arrive at the same conclusion: the consoling experiences are more clearly from God than are the disturbing doubts.

If the doubts were from God, they would lead to a deeper conversation with God, whereas what happens is that the conversation stops. In such cases, people don't talk to God about being unable to love certain people; they just beat themselves up emotionally. They may think that they are being honest, but in fact they become very self-centered. I do not believe that this is what Jesus had in mind at the Last Supper when he told his disciples to love one another, do you? Do you believe that he would be happy that his words led people to stop talking with him? I hope you don't. I would feel very badly if one of the results of reading this book were that readers stop talking with Jesus because they feel so guilty about their lack of love for certain people or their inability, even unwillingness, to forgive certain people.

If I feel that way, imagine how Jesus feels when his words lead us to stop talking with him because we feel so guilty.

The Rich Man

Maybe I can get across the point I'm trying to make here by referring you to Jesus' experience with the rich man, as told by Mark.

> As he was setting out on a journey, a man ran up and knelt before him, and asked him, "Good Teacher, what must I do to inherit eternal life?" Jesus said to him, "Why do you call me good? No one is good but God alone. You know the commandments: 'You shall not murder; You shall not commit adultery; You shall not steal; You shall not bear false witness; You shall not defraud; Honor your father and mother.'" He said to him, "Teacher, I have kept all these since my youth." Jesus, looking at him, loved him and said, "You lack one thing; go, sell what you own, and give the money to the poor, and you will have treasure in heaven; then come, follow me." When he heard this, he was shocked and went away grieving, for he had many possessions. (Mark 10:17–22)

Notice that Jesus looked at him and loved him. Do you think that Jesus stopped loving him as he walked away? Of course not. How do you think Jesus would have reacted if the man had returned and said, "I can't give up my wealth? Can I still stick around with you?" Would Jesus say, "I don't want to see you again until you do what I told you"? I doubt it very much, and I suspect that you do too. Well, it's the same when we can't or don't even want to love certain people. We can still keep up our friendship with Jesus. We can tell him the truth about our inability or unwillingness to love certain people. Of course, we'll never forget, after this, that he asked us to love one another, but at least we can talk with him about our difficulties in loving certain people. We can, in other words, continue to keep up our side of the friendship, openly acknowledging that we're not (yet) up to what he hopes for us.

Also, the rich man could have come back to Jesus and said, "I can't give up my wealth. Can you help me to do it? Will you stay with me as I learn how to be a better friend of yours?" What would Jesus have done? Wouldn't he have thrown his arms around him and told him he would be happy to help him? In fact, this is what people who find themselves trapped in addictions tell God when they do the Twelve Steps. In the First Step they admit they are powerless over their addiction; in the Second they come to believe that a Power greater than themselves could restore their sanity; in the Third they choose to turn their will and their lives over to the care of God as they understand him. To get back to the Gospel story, all the rich man had to do was to admit to Jesus that he couldn't give up his riches and ask his help, putting himself in Jesus' hands.

What we must remember is that God's love for us and God's desire for our sanity and our friendship never waver. God will never throw us out of the house! We will have to do that on our own, and we do it when we stop talking with God as a friend to a friend. We walk out on the friendship.

> How do you react to these thoughts? Do you want to say anything to Jesus? If so, go ahead and see how the conversation develops.

What about Hell?

You might say, "But God threatens us with hell if we don't obey the commandments." Remember what the first letter of John says: "God is love" (1 John 4:16). God never changes; God is always love. Thus, I don't believe that hell is God's choice; it's our choice. God never stops loving us; if anyone ends up finally and irrevocably refusing God's love, that person will have chosen whatever hell is, and it might be annihilation or the loss of existence altogether, for all we know. I cannot imagine God taking pleasure in that prospect. Can you?

Remember to take a break from reading or praying every now and then. When you are ready to begin again, recall the suggestions for starting any period of reading or praying.

Now, let's get back to what the Scriptures tell us about love of our neighbor, remembering that God is ever willing to help us fulfill this "command" of Jesus. The first letter of John says, "The children of God and the children of the devil are revealed in this way: all who do not do what is right are not from God, nor are those who do not love their brothers and sisters" (1 John 3:10). We demonstrate whether we are children of God by how we love our neighbor. That's daunting, isn't it? But the writer keeps up the beat: "All who hate a brother or sister are murderers, and you know that murderers do not have eternal life abiding in them. We know love by this, that he laid down his life for us—and we ought to lay down our lives for one another. How does God's love abide in anyone who has the world's goods and sees a brother or sister in need and yet refuses help?" (1 John 3:15–17). I cringe when I let these words sink in. Do you?

Remember what we have just reflected on before this section. No matter what our reactions are, we can tell them to our friend Jesus and to his—and our—dear Father. You can tell him that you cringe when you hear these words, especially if the words remind you of someone or even many whom you do not love and perhaps don't want to love. We can tell our friend the worst things about ourselves and expect that God will still love us and will try to help us to become better persons.

The Second Step of A.A. states, "Came to believe that a Power greater than ourselves could restore us to sanity." An alcoholic, you see, believes that he cannot live without a drink. To believe that is to live in an unreal world, to be insane. Alcohol not only is not necessary for life but for alcoholics it's unhealthy for life. Sanity means living in the real world, and for alcoholics, living in the real world means avoiding the substance over which they have no control and which will kill them if they keep using it. Without God, perhaps, there is no hope for an addict, but the reality is that God exists. So, sanity is possible. Alcoholics believe that God can help them live in the real world and thus restore them to sanity. I have come to the conviction that the first three Steps of A.A. can help all of us live in the real world. Bear with me as I ask you to follow my reasoning on this point.

Earlier we prayed and reflected on the creation stories of Genesis. According to these stories, we are made in the image and likeness of God. We also prayed and reflected on who

God is and read repeatedly that God is love, compassion, mercy, and forgiveness unbounded, that God is creative and inventive and wants the flourishing of creation and that God wants human beings to cooperate in the great work of creation. This is the One in whose image we are created.

So the *real* world that God wants is one in which we human beings act as God would as a human being. When we fail to act as God would, as we so very often have done and do, we are acting against the reality of who we are; we are acting insanely, to the detriment of our own lives and those of others and ultimately to the detriment of the world we live in. Love of neighbor, we will see, is a saner way to live.

A reminder: You might need to take a break. When you are ready to continue, remember the suggestions for every session of reading or prayer mentioned earlier.

The First Letter of John

Now we may better understand the fourth chapter of John's letter, specifically 1 John 4:7–21, which gets to the heart of the matter of love of neighbor. Ask God's help to feel the rightness of what the writer says and the desire to put it into effect in your life.

Beloved, let us love one another, because love is from God; everyone who loves is born of God and knows God. Whoever does not love does not know God, for God is love. God's love was revealed among us in this way: God sent his only Son into the world so that we might live through him. In this is love, not that we loved God but that he loved us and sent his Son to be the atoning sacrifice for our sins. Beloved, since God loved us so much, we also ought to love one another. No one has ever seen God; if we love one another, God lives in us, and his love is perfected in us. . . . God is love, and those who abide in love abide in God, and God abides in them. Love has been perfected among us in this: that we may have boldness on the day of judgment, because as he is, so are we in this world. There is no fear in love, but perfect love casts out fear; for fear has to do with punishment, and whoever fears has not reached perfection in love. We love because he first loved us. Those who say, "I love God," and hate their brothers or sisters, are liars; for those who do not love a brother or sister whom they have seen, cannot love God whom they have not seen. The commandment we have from him is this: those who love God must love their brothers and sisters also. (1 John 4:7–12, 16–21)

The writer is describing what it means to be a sane human being in this world. He clearly knows the Bible's creation story. He underlines who God is: "God is love, and those who abide in love abide in God, and God abides in them." This reminds us of Jesus' prayer at the end of the Last Supper in John's Gospel, doesn't it? Just as Jesus and the Father are one in love, so too, Jesus prays, we are to be one in love with them. Remember our earlier reflections on this real world: it is shot through with God's love, with the oneness of Father, Son, and Holy Spirit, a unity of love that keeps creating this world and holding it in existence. When we act as images of God, we love one another and live in the real world. We are sane, in other words, when we abide in love, because the real world is shot through with God who is love.

I urge you to read these words of 1 John over and over and to beg God to help you to live as a human being. And while you are begging God for yourself, say a prayer for me and for all your brothers and sisters in the world. For the sake of our world all of us need to become sane. God, in infinite mercy and compassion, has chosen to create a world in which God's dream in creation depends on our acting as images of God. You might want to ask Jesus' help to notice where you have seen God's dream actually occurring in your life or in the world around you. You might be surprised at how often people, even people you would never expect it from, do act as images of God.

A reminder: Take a break when you need one. And when you are ready to move on, remember the suggestions for every session of reading and/or prayer.

The Sermon on the Mount

So far in this section, we have concentrated on the writings ascribed to John. The injunction to love our neighbor is, however, not limited to this writer. In the Sermon on the Mount in Matthew's Gospel, for example, we read some powerful statements by Jesus that repeat some of the injunctions of the Old Testament and then raise the ante. In this section of Matthew's Gospel, Jesus is portrayed as the new Moses, the new interpreter of God's message. When he says "You have heard it said," he is referring to prior interpretations of the Mosaic law. In each case, he gives his own authoritative interpretation. Here are some examples.

> You have heard that it was said to those of ancient times, "You shall not murder"; and "whoever murders shall be liable to judgment." But I say to you that if you are angry with a brother or sister, you will be liable to judgment; and if you insult a brother or sister, you will be liable to

the council; and if you say, "You fool," you will be liable to the hell of fire. (Matthew 5:21–22)

You have heard that it was said, "An eye for an eye and a tooth for a tooth." But I say to you, Do not resist an evildoer. But if anyone strikes you on the right cheek, turn the other also; and if anyone wants to sue you and take your coat, give your cloak as well; and if anyone forces you to go one mile, go also the second mile. Give to everyone who begs from you, and do not refuse anyone who wants to borrow from you. (Matthew 5:38–42)

You have heard that it was said, "You shall love your neighbor and hate your enemy." But I say to you, Love your enemies and pray for those who persecute you, so that you may be children of your Father in heaven; for he makes his sun rise on the evil and on the good, and sends rain on the righteous and on the unrighteous. For if you love those who love you, what reward do you have? Do not even the tax collectors do the same? And if you greet only your brothers and sisters, what more are you doing than others? Do not even the Gentiles do the same? Be perfect, therefore, as your heavenly Father is perfect. (Matthew 5:43–48)

How did you react to these passages? If you let these words of Jesus sink in, you will never again accept any statement that contrasts the Old Testament God with the New Testament God. The Abba, "loving Father," of Jesus is Yahweh, the Compassionate One, of the Old Testament. In the passages we just read, Jesus makes clear what should have been clear to all readers of the Old Testament, namely, that God is the dear Father of every human being ever created, including the ones the Israelites regarded as enemies. You may want to tell Jesus about your reactions. If you do, remember to wait to see if he responds.

When Jesus says that you should not resist an evildoer and then goes on to illustrate what he means, he is most likely talking about what a Roman soldier, one of the often-cruel occupiers of Israel, might do: slap you in the face or demand that you carry his baggage a mile. Jesus takes it a bit further by quoting the line "You shall love your neighbor and hate your enemy" and then saying, "But I say to you, Love your enemies and pray for those who persecute you." He's talking about the Roman occupiers and other functionaries who crucified anyone who rebelled against their authority, who taxed them unmercifully, who demeaned them at every turn, who even defiled the temple, the holiest shrine of Israel. Jesus is talking not about some nameless and vague enemy of his hearers but about the real ones that impinged on their lives, often enough in cruel and demeaning ways. So, as you pray over these lines, make sure that you put real faces and names to the words *enemies* and *evildoers*.

By the way, if you find that there are some people you can't even pray for, here's a suggestion. Admit to Jesus that you can't pray for these people and see how he reacts. Can you ask for his help to be able to pray for them? If so, do it. If not, tell him you can't even do that. Then see if you can ask him to give you the desire to pray for them. In other words, don't walk away from the relationship with Jesus, no matter what your reactions are. Keep talking to him honestly. He can take it, I assure you. He's heard a lot worse and stayed friends with those who said far worse. Remember that he washed the feet of Judas, trying up to the last moment to keep him close.

The Clincher for Jesus

At the end of the passages we just read, Jesus delivers what, for him, is the clincher for his interpretation of the Mosaic law: "Be perfect, therefore, as your heavenly Father is perfect" (Matthew 5:48). *That's impossible,* I hear you say, and I agree, if we take the word *perfect* as meaning without sin or any imperfection. But remember that Jesus had a very good knowledge of human frailty and sinfulness. Remember also that he is not interested in placing impossible burdens on our shoulders. What he asks here must be within our capabilities. Jesus knows that in the beginning, God creates us in the image and likeness of God. Therefore, it must be within our capabilities to love our neighbor as ourselves. Why not understand Jesus as saying, "be the images of God you were created to be"? In addition, Jesus promised that after his resurrection he would send the Holy Spirit to help us to be who we are created to be.

A reminder: Take a break when you have been reading and praying for some time. When you are ready to continue, remember the suggestions for beginning any new period of reading and prayer. Then continue to the following section.

The Elder Zosima's Wisdom

Some prayerful reflections on a scene in Dostoevsky's novel *The Brothers Karamazov* might help you in your desire to live more as a person made in God's image. In this story, we are introduced to the saintly, and sickly, Elder Zosima. Many people come to seek wisdom from him. In one scene, a wealthy young widow with a crippled daughter seeks his advice. She tends to chatter on at great length, but at one point she professes her lack of faith in life after death, which she can't prove. This gives Zosima a chance to get a word in. He agrees that it can't be proven but says that it is possible to be convinced. "How?" she asks, and he responds,

> By the experience of active love. Try to love your neighbors actively and tirelessly. The more you succeed in loving, the more you'll be convinced of the existence of God and the immortality of your soul. And if you reach complete selflessness in the love of your neighbor, then

undoubtedly you will believe and no doubt will even be able to enter your soul. This has been tested. It is certain. (56)

Zosima tells the widow that she will become convinced of God's existence and of her own immortality by action, the action of loving her neighbors. He says that intellectual proofs won't help at all with the most important questions we face in life, but active love will lead to the kind of real peace of mind and heart we seek. He ends a long discussion with the widow with these words.

Never be frightened of your own faintheartedness in attaining love, and meanwhile do not even be very frightened by your own bad acts. I am sorry that I cannot say anything more comforting, for active love is a harsh and fearful thing compared to love in dreams. Love in dreams thirsts for immediate action, quickly performed, and with everyone watching. Indeed, it will go as far as the giving even of one's life, provided it does not take long but is soon over, as on stage, and everyone is looking on and praising. Whereas active love is labor and perseverance, and for some people, perhaps, a whole science. But I predict that even in that very moment when you see with horror that despite all your efforts, you not only have not come nearer your goal but seem to have gotten farther from it, at that very moment—I predict this to you—you will suddenly reach your goal and will clearly behold over you the wonder-working power of the Lord, who all the while has been loving you, and all the while has been mysteriously guiding you. (58)

This is a profound passage that needs prayerful reflection. As you do that reflection, recall how you have felt when you have acted unselfishly for someone else. You may also remember seeing how happy unselfish people seem to be. Dorothy Day, the cofounder of the Catholic Worker movement in the 1930s, worked tirelessly with and for the poor in New York City and was, by all accounts, a deeply serene and happy woman. Her favorite line was "Love in action is a harsh and dreadful thing," another translation of the line from Dostoevsky above.

If you do reflect prayerfully on this passage, recall that active love means love shown in deeds. It is a harsh and dreadful thing, for it is so hard to do. All of us have affinities with this widow. We do want to be noticed for our good deeds, and we do resent people who are not grateful to us for what we do for them. But we are made in the image and likeness of God, who loves in action and does not count the cost or withhold love if there is no gratitude.

Our response of gratitude is not required, but it is appreciated, I'm sure. However, God does not change when we do not show our gratitude. God is love, without any qualifiers. God's love does not depend on our response in any way. It just is. The response of gratitude is a sign of our sanity—our recognition of what is true and real—and is necessary for our happiness. It is also a sign of our love for God. Notice that this woman is not a happy woman, nor will she be happy until she discovers, as Zosima notes, that God has finally overcome her fears and self-absorption so that she can be both grateful for what she has in life and able to love in action.

Perhaps you can, once again, make the following prayer your own. It is taken from volume IV of *The Liturgy of the Hours* for the 28th Sunday in Ordinary Time.

> Lord, our help and our guide, make your love the foundation of our lives. May our love for you express itself in our eagerness to do good for others. Grant this through our Lord Jesus Christ, your Son, who lives and reigns with you and the Holy Spirit, one God, for ever and ever.

The lovely hymn "For the Beauty of the Earth" will make a fitting end for this session since it celebrates in one stanza "the joy of human love." The hymn was written by Folliott S. Pierpoint (1835–1917).

> For the beauty of the earth,
> For the beauty of the skies,

For the love which from our birth
Over and around us lies,
(Refrain)
Lord of all, to thee we raise
This our hymn of grateful praise.

For the beauty of each hour
Of the day and of the night,
Hill and vale, and tree and flower,
Sun and moon and stars of light.
(Refrain)

For the joy of human love,
Brother, sister, parent, child,
Friends on earth, and friends above,
For all gentle thoughts and mild,
(Refrain)

For each perfect gift of thine
To our race so freely given,
Graces human and divine,
Flow'rs of earth and buds of heaven,
(Refrain)

PART 7

WHO IS MY NEIGHBOR?

In Luke's Gospel, a lawyer tested Jesus by asking, "What must I do to inherit eternal life?" Jesus turned the tables by asking him to answer, and he promptly named the two great commandments as the way to eternal life. Then, to justify himself before the crowd, the lawyer asked Jesus, "Who is my neighbor?" Jesus responded with the great story of the Good Samaritan. As you read and pray over this story, remember that Samaritans were sworn enemies of the Israelites and worshipped God not in Jerusalem but on their own holy mountain. Remember, too, the suggestions for beginning any period of reading or prayer.

> Jesus replied, "A man was going down from Jerusalem to Jericho, and fell into the hands of robbers, who stripped him, beat him, and went away, leaving him half dead.

Now by chance a priest was going down that road; and when he saw him, he passed by on the other side. So likewise a Levite, when he came to the place and saw him, passed by on the other side. But a Samaritan while traveling came near him; and when he saw him, he was moved with pity. He went to him and bandaged his wounds, having poured oil and wine on them. Then he put him on his own animal, brought him to an inn, and took care of him. The next day he took out two denarii, gave them to the innkeeper, and said, 'Take care of him; and when I come back, I will repay you whatever more you spend.' Which of these three, do you think, was a neighbor to the man who fell into the hands of the robbers?" He said, "The one who showed him mercy." Jesus said to him, "Go and do likewise." (Luke 10:29–37)

Jesus doesn't react angrily to the lawyer's testing question or start an argument about the meaning of *neighbor*. That's our tendency, not his. He just tells a story about a man who was mugged on the road between Jerusalem and Jericho, a stretch of road everyone knew was dangerous because of robbers. My presumption is that he was a Jew. Three men come down the road and see the wounded man. All of them must have some feelings of compassion for the man, and all may wonder if he is still alive and needs help. Two of them, a priest and a Levite, both Jews themselves, cross the road to pass him by. We are not told why they avoid him. Jesus leaves it to his hearers to speculate on that matter. The main thing is, they don't help this man who is in deep trouble.

A Samaritan, whom Jews consider an enemy, sees the mugged man, is moved with compassion ("pity" in this translation), and goes out of his way to help his enemy. Then Jesus asks the question, "Which of these three, do you think, was a neighbor to the man who fell into the hands of the robbers?" In effect, Jesus asks the lawyer, "If you were the mugged man, whom would you want as a neighbor?" For Jesus, the neighbor is the person who acts on his feelings of compassion and cares for the wounded man. The Samaritan acts as a person made in God's image.

Jesus shows no interest in theorizing about the question of who the neighbor is; for him, the question is, whom would you want as a neighbor when you are in trouble? Jesus' story may give us an answer to what it means to love our neighbor as ourselves. Here we are faced with what we would want someone to do for us if we were hurt on the side of the road. Jesus tells us to act as we would want someone to act toward us.

Were you able to imagine this story? How did you react to the mugged man? To the priest and the Levite? To the Samaritan? Did you sense how the injured man reacted to each of the people who came by? You can talk to Jesus about these reactions. That might start a conversation with him. See how it develops. It might help if you spent time imagining yourself in some difficulty when you would need the help of someone else. Think, for instance, of having a flat tire on a rainy night on a highway when you forgot your cell phone. Cars are whizzing by. What do you want someone to do? Then, perhaps, when you see someone in a similar situation, you will be more likely to stop to offer help. All of us are made in the image of God; thus, all of us, unless we are depraved, are moved by the plight of another human being in trouble. The question is how we will respond to being moved.

A Disclaimer, Again

I want to repeat my purpose in writing this book. I am not trying to convince readers that they should love God and neighbor. That's taken for granted by any Christian or Jew or even any believer in a personal God who creates the universe. Rather, I am interested in proposing ways for us to grow into the human beings God creates us to be, people who *do* love God and their neighbor. Anyone who picks up a book like this wants to be such a person, but we often don't know how to grow into that person or even if it's possible to do it. I believe it's possible, which is why I encourage you, the reader, to allow these stories and your own honest responses to them to do their work in your heart and mind.

I'm hoping to help you grow into greater love for God and neighbor and thus live out who you truly are as a person made in God's image. I've tried not to badger you but to give you ways to approach Scripture and other reading that might help you become who you want to become. I want to continue that approach in this section on love of neighbor. If you begin to think I am trying to push you, give me the benefit of the doubt, and assume that I am trying to suggest ways to let God do whatever convincing is done.

Our Neighbor as Ourselves

The second great commandment asks us to love our neighbor as ourselves. We take the "as ourselves" for granted, but do we know what it means to love ourselves?

Concentration on self sounds like narcissism, doesn't it? Narcissists, however, are people who don't really love themselves; they seem to need the adulation of others to convince themselves that they are beloved. If they could be convinced of the love of even one person, they might be able to care for others, not to win them over but just because the other needs such care. In retreats and spiritual direction, I spend time with people, helping them experience God's love for them so that they then grow in love for God. It's only when we are convinced by experience that we are loved by God that we can face the issue of our sin and really grasp what sin is, a slap in the face of Someone who loves us passionately and whom we love.

In Psalm 139 I find an example of how this dynamic works. If you read that psalm, you will find that in it, you are praising and thanking God for having made you with such loving care and concern. Finally, in the last lines, the psalmist can say honestly to God,

> Search me, O God, and know my heart;
>   test me and know my thoughts.
> See if there is any wicked way in me,
>   and lead me in the way everlasting.
> (Psalm 139:23–24)

In these final verses, the psalmist, knowing God's love for him, can now ask God to show him where he has strayed from and offended God. Because I believe that love for God will more likely lead to love for neighbor, I have spent a lot of time in this book giving you ways to experience God's *love for you* and thus increase your response of love for God.

To love anyone else means to have some empathy for the person, some ability to walk around in that person's shoes, to feel for him or her. This includes the ability and willingness to see the other person not as a member of a certain category but as a unique person whose mystery we approach with reverence. Such empathy may be inborn; it may be the result of being created in the image and likeness of God. I vaguely remember reading about some studies of very young children that indicate that they do reach out to other children in trouble. It would not surprise me that we are so wired from birth, but such natural tendencies to care for others need nurturing, which comes only from feeling cared for (loved) ourselves. Does this make sense to you? Does it match your experience?

Lurking over my shoulder for the past few days of writing has been the thought of the many people who find themselves addicted to being a helper and who join such organizations as Co-Dependents Anonymous. For such people, loving their neighbor often comes at the expense of not taking care of themselves.

The command to love our neighbor as ourselves needs to be nuanced so that it is not used to enable co-dependent people to continue in behavior that is detrimental to themselves and probably not ultimately helpful to those they care for. An example might be the relative of an alcoholic who won't believe there is a problem and who keeps providing the alcoholic with the help that feeds the addiction. The second great commandment does not condone, let alone encourage, such behavior.

What Does God Mean by Loving Our Neighbor as Ourselves?

As I pondered this issue of loving my neighbor as myself, I remembered that this is God's teaching and wondered, *What does God mean by telling us to love our neighbor as ourselves?* Perhaps God wants us to love ourselves as God loves self. This would follow through on the fact that we are made in the image and likeness of God. It seems pretty logical, but does it help us at all, given that God is mystery itself? Perhaps we can do some prayerful reflection on it together.

> May I ask you, then, to join me in asking God, "Help us to understand what it might mean for us to love ourselves as you love yourself." (I confess that right now I don't know how this prayerful reflection will end. So we are in the same boat.)

One thing hits me immediately: God is not self-absorbed in love for self, even though God does love self. Within God's one being is a unity of three who are one God. Father, Son, and Holy Spirit are united in love of one another. God's love of self is already relational, in some mysterious way. But that love is not self-absorbed. Divine love freely moves out to create, at the least, our universe with all that is in it, and also to send the Son to become a human being in order to save us from ourselves. God does not lose self in loving the created universe. Perhaps it might even be that God's self-love reaches perfection in freely creating what is not God—everything else that exists.

I find that I am happiest and most myself when I choose to love others unselfishly; I do this freely, but it also seems to be what I am created to be and do. Have you noticed how happy you are when you love others unselfishly, your spouse or children, for example? Could it be that such selfless human love is a pale image of divine love that freely reaches perfection by pouring itself out in creating what is not God?

Many people find they are most themselves when they love others unselfishly; they speak of being most happy when they are caring for others. Moreover, some psychological studies have shown that people who care for others are the happiest people. It would be strange indeed if acting as a person made in God's image were to lead to being very unhappy; perhaps we have hit on something fundamental about what it means to love others as ourselves: genuine self-love leads freely to the love of others.

Before we move on, it might be a good idea to take a break to let the reflection of the last few paragraphs sink in and to see if it holds water over time.

I've come back to the book the day after writing the last couple of paragraphs. In the interim, I have felt that God was with me as I wrote. I have just reread them, and they still ring true. I did make some changes, but these were not in meaning, only in the expressions. I still sense that we touched on something profound about God and about ourselves in that section. What were your reactions as you prayed and reflected on the paragraphs?

Happiness Comes from Caring for Others

The following reflection on the Beatitudes in Matthew's Gospel may bolster this point about growing in happiness as a result of being made in God's image. As you begin this section, recall the suggestions for beginning any period of prayer. Matthew's Sermon on the Mount begins with the Beatitudes:

> When Jesus saw the crowds, he went up the mountain; and after he sat down, his disciples came to him. Then he began to speak, and taught them, saying:
>
> Blessed are the poor in spirit, for theirs is the kingdom of heaven.
>
> Blessed are those who mourn, for they will be comforted.
>
> Blessed are the meek, for they will inherit the earth.

> Blessed are those who hunger and thirst for righteousness, for they will be filled.
>
> Blessed are the merciful, for they will receive mercy.
>
> Blessed are the pure in heart, for they will see God.
>
> Blessed are the peacemakers, for they will be called children of God.
>
> Blessed are those who are persecuted for righteousness' sake, for theirs is the kingdom of heaven.
>
> Blessed are you when people revile you and persecute you and utter all kinds of evil against you falsely on my account. Rejoice and be glad, for your reward is great in heaven, for in the same way they persecuted the prophets who were before you. (Matthew 5:1–12)

What are we to make of these beatitudes as the opening salvo of Jesus' teaching about the kingdom of God? A lot depends on how you translate the Greek word *makarios*, which is here translated in the usual way as "blessed." The word can also mean "happy," which puts a different spin on these sayings. "Happy are the poor," "those who mourn," "the meek," "the merciful," etc., ending with "Happy are you when people revile you and persecute you and utter all kinds of evil against you falsely on my account." In his translation of the New Testament, Tom Wright makes an even sharper point by translating the word *makarios* as "Wonderful news." Listen again to these opening words in his translation.

Wonderful news for the poor in spirit! The kingdom of heaven is yours. Wonderful news for the mourners! You're going to be comforted. Wonderful news for the meek! You're going to inherit the earth. Wonderful news for people who hunger and thirst for God's justice! You're going to be satisfied. Wonderful news for the merciful! You'll receive mercy yourselves. Wonderful news for the pure in heart! You will see God. Wonderful news for the peacemakers! You'll be called God's children. Wonderful news for people who are persecuted because of God's way. The kingdom of heaven belongs to you. Wonderful news for you, when people slander you and persecute you, and say all kinds of wicked things about you falsely because of me! Celebrate and rejoice: there's great reward for you in heaven. That's how they persecuted the prophets who went before you. (34)

This translation, it seems to me, gets to the heart of what Jesus is about in his life and teaching. He really is gospel, "Good News": "I'm here to tell you that you are going to be very happy indeed." He's either a charlatan or crazy—or he is what he says he is: God's great gift of Godself to this world for its final healing and salvation. We believe the latter, don't we? Perhaps we have in these words of Jesus another sign that our real happiness lies in loving God and neighbor, no matter what it may cost us in pain and suffering.

The Heart of Jesus' Message

The late Brian Doyle, in his inimitable style, gets at the heart of what Jesus is telling us in the Sermon on the Mount. Read this paragraph prayerfully.

More and more as I shuffle through this vale of wonders I begin to see that humility is the final frontier. We spend so much of our early lives building person and confidence and career and status that it takes a looooong while before we sense the wild genius of the Beatitudes—blessed are those who do not think they are cool, blessed are those who abjure power, blessed are those who deflate their own arrogance and puncture their own pomposity, blessed are those who quietly try to shrive their sins without calling attention to their overweening piety, blessed are those who know they are dunderheads but forge on cheerfully anyway. The thin Jewish mystic, as usual, was pointing in the complete other direction than the arc of human history. Sprint *away* from being important, famous, powerful.

The weak are strong, mercy is greater than justice, power is powerless. *Believe in the unbelievable*, isn't that what He is saying? Isn't it? Don't try to make sense of it. Be attentive and humble and naked in spirit. Try for lean and clean though the world roars for glitter and gold. Feed the hungry, clothe the naked, succor the sick and frightened and lonely, as the Christos says later in this very gospel: *that is* the inarguable assignment, the blunt mission statement, the clear map coordinates. *That* is what we are here for: to bring love like a searing weapon against the dark, and to do so without fanfare and applause, without a care for sneers. Do what you know to be right, though the world calls you a fool? Yes! Thank you! Yes!

In the opening lines of the Sermon on the Mount, Jesus both announces wonderful news and asks us to believe in what sounds unbelievable. He is telling us, all of us, "Trust me! You're really going to be happy." Actually, this is what God has always promised us: that our real happiness lies in trusting God and living as God's images and likenesses. Why not speak to God about your reactions? It might lead to a longer conversation.

A reminder: Take a break from reading and praying.

When you're ready, your love for neighbor might find energy and inspiration in some examples of people who attest to joy in loving their neighbor, sometimes under difficult circumstances. I remind you of the suggestions for beginning any new period of reading and praying.

Dr. James J. O'Connell, founder of Boston Health Care for the Homeless Program, wrote *Stories from the Shadows: Reflections of a Street Doctor,* in which he tells stories of the work of that organization. I found it a hard book to put down, strange to say, since almost all the men and women discussed in the book die too young. Dr. O'Connell notes that "caring for the homeless has been my full-time job for more than fifteen years." This job takes him out on the streets of Boston night after night to care for men and women who are down and out. It is a labor of love; readers come to care for these men and women because their doctor clearly loves them, foibles, addictions, craziness, and all. After writing the sentence quoted above about his full-time job, he continues,

> I suspect that the joy I find in my job bespeaks a deep character flaw, a subject I puzzle over often with my close friend and hero, Pedro Jose Greer . . . who noted [paraphrasing Yeats] that the Irish are a people whose sense of impending tragedy and guilt has remained constant throughout the centuries despite brief moments of unmitigated joy. While this essay could no doubt plumb the tragedy, I would prefer to seize the joy. (88)

For all I know, O'Connell may have a deep character flaw; if so, it's one I would be happy to share. I'm sure that, like all of us, he has his idiosyncrasies. Nonetheless, he's the kind of man I would be happy to call a friend, if I were that lucky. And his book, despite the heartache that reading it entailed, was for me a spiritual tonic. It's written by a very happy man.

Another example of someone who finds himself happiest when he is trying to help others is Darrell Jones, an African American who was sentenced to life in prison without parole for a murder he did not commit. His conviction has now been overturned, thank God, after Darrell spent thirty-two years in prison. Of course, he gets angry when he reflects on what happened to him and how he was treated in prison, but Darrell has told me on more than one occasion that he feels happiest when he is trying to help others, whether other prisoners or the people of the neighborhoods where he used to live. The grace of God was working overtime in prison, I think. Darrell was not always so concerned for others, but when he began to care for a woman who visited him, he realized that he could not continue to live only for himself. Her care for him was the catalyst for his conversion. He began to read the Bible and to take its stories and commands seriously. He now loves God and his neighbor to the point where he even wants to be able to forgive those who got him wrongly convicted.

Have you noticed how you feel when you are doing things for others, especially for those in great need? If you haven't noticed, perhaps you will begin to pay attention to how different you feel when you are self-centered than when you are more concerned about others. I believe that we are happiest and most ourselves when we are unselfconsciously caring for others. The reason? When we are unselfconsciously thinking of others, we are most like God. Then we are living as the people God created us to be, and we are at our sanest and happiest. What do you think of that? Perhaps you want to have a conversation with Jesus about your reactions to this section.

A reminder: Take a break if you have been reading and praying for some time. If you do take a break at this point, remember the suggestions for beginning any new period of reading and praying. Perhaps the following reflections and texts might be helpful to your prayer and desire to love your neighbor.

I have said that we are at our sanest when we are living as people made in God's image. I'm not advocating love of neighbor as a way to become sane. Anyone who engages in "love of neighbor" so as to become saner does not really love neighbor but self. Mind you, such behavior is better than hate of neighbor, but it's too self-serving to be godlike behavior. Loving one's neighbor may lead to greater happiness and sanity, but that's not the motive, at least not the primary motive, for loving your neighbor. The primary motive is love itself. What do you think?

In the Sermon on the Mount in Matthew's Gospel, Jesus tells us that we should love our enemies and pray for those who persecute us, "so that you may be children of your Father in heaven; for he makes his sun rise on the evil and on the good, and sends rain on the righteous and on the unrighteous" (Matthew 5:44–45). The motivation Jesus appeals to seems to be our love of God and desire to be like him. Jesus ends this passage with these words: "Be perfect, therefore, as your heavenly Father is perfect" (Matthew 5:48). In effect, Jesus says that we are to love as God loves, and God loves the good and the bad; God loves Mary, the mother of Jesus, and God loves Judas Iscariot, God loves St. Teresa of Calcutta, and God loves Adolph Hitler. The motivation Jesus appeals to is our love for God and God's love for all of us sinners, even the worst people we know.

Remember what we reflected on in session #13, that Jesus died for the unjust as well as for the just, for the evilest reprobate as well as for the garden-variety sinner. As Christopher Smart wrote in the hymn cited near the end of that section, Jesus has "those feet still free to move and bleed / for millions, / and for me." Remember, too, how we began these sessions on love for neighbor by reflecting prayerfully on Jesus' words and actions at the Last Supper in John's Gospel. There we saw how, again and again, Jesus stressed his love for his friends and begged them to love one another, and how he prayed in chapter 17 of John's Gospel for all of us, that we might be one in love with him and the Father. The biggest motivation for us to love our neighbor is twofold: God's almost unbelievably forgiving and compassionate love for each one of us, sinners though we all are, and our love for such a loving God.

The Hymn to Jesus in Paul's Context

The apostle Paul often appeals to God's love for us when he exhorts his Christian communities to love one another. In session #9 we already prayed over the hymn extolling Jesus in Paul's letter to the Philippians. At that time I suggested the passage as a way of thanking and praising Jesus for what he has done for us. But here is the whole passage. Notice that Paul uses the hymn to motivate the Philippians to love one another in very concrete ways; they are urged to imitate Jesus.

> If then there is any encouragement in Christ, any consolation from love, any sharing in the Spirit, any compassion and sympathy, make my joy complete: be of the same mind, having the same love, being in full accord and of one mind. Do nothing from selfish ambition or conceit,

but in humility regard others as better than yourselves. Let each of you look not to your own interests, but to the interests of others. Let the same mind be in you that was in Christ Jesus,

who though he was in the form of God,
   did not regard equality with God
   as something to be exploited,
but emptied himself,
   taking the form of a slave,
   being born in human likeness.
And being found in human form,
   he humbled himself
   and became obedient to the point of death—
   even death on a cross.
Therefore God also highly exalted him
   and gave him the name
   that is above every other name,
so that at the name of Jesus
   every knee should bend,
   in heaven and on earth and under the earth,
and every tongue should confess
   that Jesus Christ is Lord,
   to the glory of God the Father. (Philippians 2:1–11)

Let this passage sink into your heart and soul. Try to pray it aloud and notice how you react, and then speak to Jesus and to the Father.

Let me also suggest that you reflect prayerfully again on these words from the first letter of John.

God is love, and those who abide in love abide in God, and God abides in them. Love has been perfected among us in this: that we may have boldness on the day of judgment, because as he is, so are we in this world. There is no fear in love, but perfect love casts out fear; for fear has to do with punishment, and whoever fears has not reached perfection in love. We love because he first loved us. Those who say, "I love God," and hate their brothers or sisters, are liars; for those who do not love a brother or sister whom they have seen, cannot love God whom they have not seen. The commandment we have from him is this: those who love God must love their brothers and sisters also. (1 John 4:16–21)

It's pretty plain, isn't it? "We love because he first loved us." For the writer of this letter, everything begins and ends in the love of God, a God who is madly in love with everything he creates. And remember that we are made in the image and likeness of God. Don't you want to be like God? If you feel that desire, every day before you leave home you can ask God to help you to meet everyone with the same kind of openness and warmth God has for them.

PART 8

LOVE OF THOSE CLOSE TO US

In the Sermon on the Mount, Jesus seems to presume that we will love those close to us. He says, "If you love those who love you, what reward do you have? Do not even the tax collectors do the same? And if you greet only your brothers and sisters, what more are you doing than others? Do not even the Gentiles do the same?" (Matthew 5:46–47). Jesus' real concern is how we treat those who do not love us, even those who hate us. No doubt it's easier to love those who love us, but we all know that it is sometimes hard to love those who are the closest to us. I want to look at some of these difficulties in these sections. But first, it might be helpful to look at how God has continued to love you and me even though we have deeply hurt God. This realization may help you in loving those who have hurt you.

With Everlasting Love I Will Have Compassion on You

Second Isaiah (chapters 40–55 of Isaiah) speaks to the Israelites who have been exiled to Babylon after the Babylonian armies conquered Jerusalem and destroyed the temple, the place where God had sworn to dwell with his people. It is written to a people who know that they are in exile because of their idolatry and unwillingness to trust in God. They have deeply offended God, yet the book brings words of comfort, and it promises a return from exile. In one section, God speaks in this way to this sinful and lost people:

> Do not fear, for you will not be ashamed;
>   do not be discouraged, for you will not suffer
>   disgrace;
> for you will forget the shame of your youth,
>   and the disgrace of your widowhood you will
>   remember no more.
> For your Maker is your husband,
>   the Lord of hosts is his name;
> the Holy One of Israel is your Redeemer,
>   the God of the whole earth he is called.
> For the Lord has called you
>   like a wife forsaken and grieved in spirit,
> like the wife of a man's youth when she is cast off,
>   says your God.
> For a brief moment I abandoned you,

> but with great compassion I will gather you.
> In overflowing wrath for a moment
>   I hid my face from you,
> but with everlasting love I will have compassion
>   on you,
>   says the LORD, your Redeemer. (Isaiah 54:4–8)

With varied images Isaiah tries to get across to these broken and disheartened people that God has not abandoned them. And then those lovely and consoling words: "For a brief moment I abandoned you, but with great compassion [womb-love] I will gather you. In overflowing wrath for a moment I hid my face from you, but with everlasting love I will have compassion on you, says the LORD, your Redeemer." This passage is just one of many in the Hebrew Bible that tell of God's forgiving love for those who have deeply offended him. And remember that we are made in God's image and likeness.

You might also want to recall our contemplation of the Annunciation when, with the prompting of Ignatius of Loyola, we pondered the Trinity looking down on the earth and seeing how lost and sinful we had become. Instead of calling it quits with us, God decides that the Son will become one of us. No greater love can be thought of than this great act of God becoming one of us: "God so loved the world that he gave his only Son, so that everyone who believes in him may not perish but may have eternal life" (John 3:16). And God did this even though, as Paul writes, "all have sinned and fall short of the glory of God" (Romans 3:23). Jesus died for us and in our place; that's how crazy in love with us God is.

Reconciliation in the Family

I'm sure that you can recall, as I do, instances when you have been the recipient of love and forgiveness from someone close to you whom you have deeply offended. No doubt, too, you have heard instances of how families have suffered estrangement because of something that happened at a crucial time in their history—and you have also heard of unexpected reconciliations. Here is where the rubber of love of those close to us hits the road and calls us to act as Christians. Remember the suggestions for beginning any session of prayer.

One such case of seeming estrangement and reconciliation in the wake of the U.S. election of 2016 was brought to my attention by a posting on the Web site of the Jesuit magazine *America*, December 7, 2016, by Nick Genovese, a recent graduate of Boston College and an intern at *America*. Right after the election of Donald Trump, he had posted a short article about his anger at his family's happiness about the election when he was deeply troubled. In that article he wrote hurtful things about his parents without talking to them prior to the posting. He writes:

> My words in it were harsh, angry, and bitter, and I feared they would push my parents away from me. I had meant to call them. I wanted them to hear it from me. I wanted to explain to them how I truly felt. But Facebook got to them first. Three days after the article was published online, my mom called me.
>
> "Hi, honey. We read the article that you wrote. We just wanted to know if everything is O.K.?"
>
> Before she said another word, my guilt over writing the article poured out. "I'm sorry, Mom. I wanted to write it anonymously. I didn't really mean it. I don't actually feel as strongly as it reads."
>
> Before that week, I had never said anything negative about my parents. Now, I felt like I had attacked and blindsided them in public without giving them a chance to explain themselves. I had turned my back on them, and in doing so, perhaps wounded my relationship with my parents forever. I thought they would be shocked and hurt by my words. I thought they would be angry and disappointed in my beliefs. Maybe other parents would. But not mine.
>
> The first thing my mom said was, "I love you and am so proud that you have matured to develop a different perspective than your father and I."

"Amazing article, buddy," followed my dad. "You know I'm your number one fan, Nicholas."

"Really?" was the only response I could muster.

Genovese goes on to say that, with this conversation, his parents had given him hope, which he rightly insists is not optimism, but trust in God. He ends the posting thus:

I should have voiced my feelings to my parents about the election before submitting the article for publication. But it took my parents reaching out to me for me to understand that my hope for healing our divided family is beyond myself. Just when I turned my back on my parents, they embraced me back into their open arms. My mom and dad did not care what thousands of readers and hundreds of commenters thought about them. They only wanted to tell me that no matter what I wrote or other people said, I am their beloved son.

And so it is with God. The ground of our hope is knowing that even when we turn away, God is infinitely in love with us, always reaching out to us.

We live in a country scarred by deep political, racial, and economic divisions. I don't know what to expect with the fractured landscape. I don't know how things will turn out in our society at large. But as God continues to reach toward us, I hope we can reach back to God and out to one another across the divides. Because unlike hatred, fear, and anger, hope endures.

Hope is not about what might be possible. Hope is about what is always and constantly true. I am hopeful we will soon understand who we truly are—a family undivided and a nation indivisible.

How did you react to Nick Genovese's story? Maybe it reminded you of a time when you were embraced with love and forgiveness when you had offended someone you loved. If so, then you know from experience how Nick felt. In keeping with one of the constant themes of this book, we might also want to recognize that Nick's parents (and our loved ones who treated us in the same way) acted as images of God for Nick on this occasion and perhaps on many others as well. They kept on loving their son even after he had deeply hurt them by his written words. This is what God does all the time with us. You can talk with Jesus about your reactions to this story and your own memories.

If we have been recipients of such love from others, then we know that it is possible to be an image of God and to love those close to us even when they have deeply offended us. And we need to remember that God's Spirit is always present in us, moving us to such acts of love. We can ask the help of the Spirit to help us live as images of God and thank the Spirit for times when we have received forgiving love from others.

I have been deeply moved by other examples of the kind of other-directed love shown by Nick Genovese's parents. For example, a friend of mine visited his wife in a nursing home every day of her life until she died. They would have dinner every evening, spend time together afterward, and end the evening with some shared prayer. This lasted for years. A woman I know visited her mother in a nursing home at least once every week; the mother had Alzheimer's disease and often was unable to talk or to recognize her. But her daughter visited, held her hand, told her how much she loved her, and went with her to some of the activities in the nursing home. You probably have met people like these who kept on loving and caring for a loved one when they might not have received much, if anything, in return—at least nothing anyone could see. Such people, too, are images of God in action.

If you have recalled any experiences like these, you can talk to Jesus about them and perhaps get into a conversation about the people you remembered.

We Experience God's Actions in Our World

Perhaps we experience the action of God in our world much more often than we realize. The kinds of love we have been examining are, I suspect, quite commonplace, which is not to say that they are at all insignificant. But what we are now contemplating might attune us to the presence of such commonplace but oh-so-significant instances of God's dream for creation coming true before our eyes. After all, every act of generous love, of kindness, of compassion is done by a human being acting, most often without advertizing the fact, as an image of God. And perhaps we are all the better for the inadvertence. Such acts, done just for the sake of the other without any thought of recompense or recognition, are, without doubt, unconditional love, a love that mirrors God's love for us and for all of creation. As you begin this session, remember the suggestions for beginning prayer.

One example of a hidden action of God was right in my backyard. The town of Weston, in recent years, renovated an area next to Campion Center, where I live. They created Burchard Park with four Little League baseball fields. Near one of these fields and the field house is a comfortable bench bearing a plaque with this citation: "In Memory of Marie Cort who always brought oranges for both teams." Note the "always." Marie Cort must have come to many games and "always" brought oranges for *both* teams. Think of that for a moment. Year upon year since the opening of the fields until, perhaps, her death, she bought enough oranges to satisfy at least eighteen players, and probably a few more. Ms. Cort, whether she knew it or not, was showing the impartial, active love of God for these boys who came to these fields to play ball. Her regular appearance at these games must have touched the hearts of enough people that this bench was put there to honor her memory. Don't we experience many, many such acts of random kindness every day? I believe we experience in such acts God's grace in action. The world is a better place because of people like Marie Cort, most of whom go without much recognition at all. But God is pleased and honored.

Suspicion of hidden, and, almost by definition, unsavory motivation has become so ingrained in us that we may not see how often people act as images of God. Perhaps we need to add more than a pinch of affection to the large dollop of suspicion we usually use to view our own actions and, perhaps especially, the actions of our fellow human beings.

What Use Is Love That Appears Unavailing?

During one session of spiritual direction, a woman recalled how she and her husband took care of her demented mother in her last years, all the while being unable to do anything to change the situation. She wondered what use they were to her mother. At one point, I noted that God is present all the time in such circumstances, seems unable to change the circumstances, and yet stays with all of us who suffer; perhaps what we are being asked to do is exactly what God does. Later as I prayed about this conversation, I said something like this to God: "Perhaps pain suffered with others in union with you does do something to change things for the better for the one suffering, and, indeed, for the world." I felt God's agreement with me.

I also thought, with sorrow, of the times I left people who were demented or dying because I did not think my presence meant anything to them or was less important than the presence of others who were closer to them. I missed opportunities to be with God and those people as they suffered and perhaps to be God's heart and hands and eyes. By reflecting on these missed opportunities, I now have the awareness not to let my diffidence and my fear hinder me from being there for others when it seems the natural thing to do.

Did you become aware of expressions or acts of kindness that you have witnessed or that you have done or that you have failed to do? These memories give you food for conversations with Jesus. You can also ask for help to be a better image of God in the future.

Liturgy and Sacrament

On another occasion, a man I know told me about a funeral liturgy for someone who had committed suicide. The priest, the husband of the woman being buried, and another eulogist all mentioned the elephant in the church—the issue of mental illness and suicide—and also talked about God's presence. My friend said that he felt a union of everyone in the church with God in prayer for the deceased and in prayer for one another. He found it hard to articulate. I did too, but it seemed to me that they were all caught up in the Mystery at the heart of creation, God loving all of us and suffering with all of us. I said something like this: "God fails all the time to keep us from being inhuman but never gives up. When we do have moments such as yours in the church, we often don't grasp what is happening unless, like you, we have the chance to talk with someone about the experience." Perhaps our prayerful reflections in this session will help us notice such instances of God's presence and of people responding as images of God to those they love, and indeed to anyone they meet in need. Then we will have more to talk over with God.

The Effects of Liturgy

Think about your experience of the Eucharist. When you were a child, did you most often celebrate the Eucharist on Sundays with your parents and the rest of the family? That was my own first experience, but I find it hard to recall what it was like because it was so long ago. However, I must have enjoyed it because I became an altar boy and served at the Sunday liturgy in the same parish until I entered the Jesuits a few months shy of my twentieth birthday. Clearly something was going on in me, but I haven't a clue now as to what that was.

Whatever your own experience was, did you ever think of it as helping you love the members of your family and your fellow parishioners, and indeed those you met in the course of the following week? Even though we can't recall ever thinking about this, it may well have been happening to us.

Week after week we went to these eucharistic celebrations; some of us even attended eucharistic liturgies daily. In the years before the Second Vatican Council, the Roman

Catholic liturgy was celebrated in Latin with the priest facing away from the people, and many of us followed along with the priest by reading the English translation in a missalette. That means that over the years we heard or read a good deal of the Bible, lived through the sacramental reenactment of Jesus' passion, death, and resurrection, and received the body and blood of the Lord many times, and we did this in the company often of our loved ones and always of other people. Without knowing it, perhaps, we gave God all these opportunities to transform us into the human beings God wants, images of God.

It's clearly imaginable that the continuing love we have for so many of the people of our past, especially our family members, is due in no small measure to those liturgies, among many other events. Remembering some of that history might give you things to tell God and also might move you to thank God, who has so persistently worked to help us become human beings. But let's not forget to be grateful for our parents (who took us, sometimes forcibly, to Sunday liturgy), siblings, fellow parishioners, and parish priests who celebrated with us; they all contributed to whatever humanizing of us happened through these liturgies. Here is another instance in which we might have missed the action of God in our lives and in our world and now have the chance to talk with God about these people.

Sacraments as Signs of God Acting in Our World

The liturgy is, after all, a sacrament, a visible and tangible sign of God acting in our world. Have you ever reflected prayerfully on this aspect of the Eucharist? Often what is emphasized is the transformation of bread and wine into the body and blood of Jesus our Lord. This is indeed very important, but we must not miss what God is about in this reenactment of the suffering and death of Jesus. God's desire is not exhausted in our adoration and thanksgiving; God wants us to be transformed by eating and drinking the body and blood of Jesus.

At the Last Supper, Jesus took bread and said, "Take and eat, this is my body" and then took a cup of wine and said, "Take and drink, this is my blood of the new covenant." He wants us to partake of himself so that we will become like him in the way we act in this world. Moreover, at the Eucharist we always hear the word of God, and this word is written not to give us information but to draw us into the story of God's dream for our world. God speaks to us through these words to transform us into images of God.

All seven of our sacraments are visible signs of God working in this world to transform us into images of God. They are all signs of God acting on us and in us to enable us to be God's images, friends, and helpers in the great work of creation, bringing about the kingdom of God. Thus the liturgy, like any other sacrament, aims at the transformation of the world through transforming those who celebrate it. The liturgy sends us forth to do God's work in this world, to be God's heart, hands, eyes, ears, and voice to all those we meet.

How do you react to this reflection? Do you want to say anything to God? Perhaps this prayer taken from the Liturgy of the Hours will help you to start such a conversation: "Lord God, our strength and salvation, put in us the flame of your love and make our love for you grow to a perfect love which reaches to our neighbor" (*The Liturgy of the Hours*, vol. IV, Week I, Office of Readings, Psalm Prayer, 711). Take some time to engage in conversation with God.

PART 9

WIDENING OUR CIRCLE OF CONCERN

At our daily liturgy, a Jesuit once mentioned that the hope of the Boston College student immersion program among the poor in the U.S. and in other countries is to widen the students' circle of concern. When the students immersed themselves in the lives and suffering of people much different from themselves, they would, it was hoped, return with a sense of belonging to a community much wider than what is often the rather narrow world we all live in. As a result, they might demonstrate that wider concern by how they lived after college. It occurred to me that this notion of widening our circle of concern would fit nicely as the theme of this section.

In his parable of the Good Samaritan, Jesus tried to widen the circle of concern of the Jewish lawyer who asked, "Who is my neighbor?" and of the other listeners. Remember how

Jesus told them to imagine themselves mugged on the side of the road and then to realize that the neighbor they would want would be the Samaritan, a man they considered an enemy. Jesus also tries to widen our circle of concern when he tells us to love our enemies and do good to those who hate us.

Readers of this book cannot avoid the conclusion that God creates and loves all human beings; all of us are kinfolk because all of us are sons or daughters of God. I take it for granted that we all know that God wants our circle of concern to embrace everyone we meet. But we also know that our hearts are not in tune with what God wants in many ways, including in the narrowness of our circle of concern. In this section, I offer some suggestions that might help us bring our hearts more in tune with God's dream of widening our circle of concern.

Another Burden?

I am well aware that you may already be tired of hearing that you ought to be concerned about this group and that group. Like you, I have felt overwhelmed by the onslaught of needs I should be concerned about as a Christian and a human being. I don't want to add to that overload; my purpose throughout the book has been to offer helps to grow in love for God and neighbor. I want to continue with that purpose in this section. I presume that you already have felt the pressure to widen your circle of concern. Let me, then, indicate some prayerful reflections that might help you deal with this pressure that our world's needs are placing on you and me without feeling overburdened and anxious. Remember the suggestions for beginning any period of prayer.

Who Is My Neighbor?

Let me begin this section with a scenario that most of us have faced. James Martin, SJ, perhaps the best-known spiritual writer in the United States at this time, tells this one on himself. He was in Rome on business for *America*, the Jesuit magazine he helps edit. He was walking from one meeting to another when a beggar asked him for a sandwich. Martin looked at his wallet and realized that he had only 20-euro notes, "a little steep for me." So he excused himself and kept walking. The beggar kept following with *Panini, Panini*. Martin says that he got angry, annoyed that he was being inconvenienced this way. He continues:

> Then it dawned on me. You idiot! Why are you in Rome? Why are you even a Christian? To see beautiful churches? To see a movie? What's the most important thing you could do right now?

So I checked my anger, which was not coming from God, and asked the man to follow me.

Inside a bakery near St. Peter's, my new friend pointed to a sandwich behind a glass case, and we waited. The line was interminable, and my anger returned. Again, I realized how un-Christian I was being. I had barely spoken to him. So I said, "*Come si chiama?*" What's your name?

"Lorenzo," he said quietly.

I almost cried when I heard it. I remembered the story of St. Lawrence (Lorenzo), the third-century archdeacon of Rome who was charged with caring for the church's financial resources. When the Emperor Valerian . . . ordered Lawrence to bring him the "riches of the church," Lawrence . . . did something surprising. He brought in the poor of Rome and told the emperor, "Here are the riches of the church."

That's who was standing beside me, I realized.

That story might help us respond in a more Christian way the next time we are approached by a beggar. At least we could look the person in the eye and say something to acknowledge his or her existence. Maybe this story will also give you something to talk about with Jesus.

Your Neighbors

Let's start with those who live close to us, our physical neighbors. In many places in the United States, we seem to have lost a sense of neighborliness. Gated communities have sprung up all over the country, especially in the suburbs of our large cities. But even in our cities, neighbors don't seem to know one another at all well.

What has been your experience in your neighborhood recently? Do you wish that you knew your neighbors better? Perhaps here is a place you may want to widen your circle of concern. What can you do?

For a few minutes or more, you could imagine Jesus with you at your kitchen table. Have a chat with him about your neighbors. If you know some of them a bit, you could tell him how you feel toward them and see how he reacts. You may notice that you wish you knew one or two of them better; if so, talk to him about how to get to know them better. The two of you may hit upon a way of breaking the ice with your neighbors.

You may also notice that you don't particularly like some of your neighbors. You might tell Jesus what you don't like, what ticks you off, and see what his reactions are. As a result of these talks with Jesus, you may come up with ways of widening your circle of concern among them and maybe even how to overcome some of the dislikes.

Years ago, when a group of Jesuits moved into a neighborhood of Cambridge, Massachusetts, we noticed that we had met only the people next door to us, yet the neighboring houses were rather close together. That first year, we decided to cook a Thanksgiving dinner for our Jesuit community and expected to have much leftover turkey. One member suggested that we make a turkey casserole and invite our neighbors to come for lunch the Sunday after Thanksgiving. We let the people around us know, and several families accepted our offer. The ice was broken. We greeted one another and, after that, sometimes had longer conversations with neighbors. During the blizzard of 1978, some of us in the neighborhood helped one another dig out so that we could park cars and walk on the sidewalks. Perhaps you can talk with members of your own household about how to break the ice with neighbors.

If we do widen our circle of concern at least to people in our neighborhood, then we can offer help when we notice that they are in trouble. It's sad when someone in a neighborhood gets sick or loses a loved one and no one in the neighborhood even knows or seems to care.

Here's a true story that still moves me. As she was getting ready to go to the gym one morning, Clara, a widow I know, noticed an ambulance outside a neighbor's house. Within minutes, a gurney was wheeled out the front door and Joe, the husband, was being lifted into the ambulance. Clara knew that Joe had a heart condition and had been slowing down lately, so she feared the worst. Instead of continuing to the gym, she went over to see if she could help Joe's wife, Mary. Mary was talking frantically on the phone to her daughters, who were on vacation in Florida. The daughters made plans to take the next flight home.

Then Mary explained to Clara that Joe seemed unconscious and so she called 911. She didn't know what else to do or how she could get to the hospital. Clara offered to take her. Joe died before they got to the hospital, but within minutes of their arrival, their parish priest also arrived to pray with them. Clara stayed with Mary until they took Joe's body away, and she then brought her back to her home. Later in the day, Clara went back to Mary's house to see how she was. Through her tears Mary said, "I called 911, and God sent me you."

When Clara told me the story, she said, "Mary's life had, once again, been changed forever. But so had mine, because soon after that, I began my funeral ministry at my parish." When we do reach out to a neighbor, we join God in the great work of creation. Our action changes us and our world, thus making the world more like what God dreams for it. Have you been reminded of anything similar that happened in your own life? Do you want to talk to God about anything at this point?

An Example of How to Defuse Difficult Situations

Earlier I mentioned the general state of anger and polarization evident in our country. We run the risk of losing all sense of living together in a commonwealth, to use the word Massachusetts and some other states use instead of "state of . . ." God has given us this world as our common wealth; none of us has created the world we inhabit together, and all of us are asked by God to help take care of this common wealth. The term is a good one to use for any government, especially one proclaimed a democracy. But how do we deal with our anger that so often devolves into debates that have no ending except mutual recrimination? We can do better. An article in the May 1, 2017, issue of *America*, the biweekly published by the Jesuits of the United States, uses the example of testimony given by Mr. Rogers, the founder of *Mr. Rogers' Neighborhood*, in 1969 before the Senate Subcommittee on Communications. Rogers is arguing for the funding of public television and especially for his own program. He looks straight at Senator John Pastore, the chair of the committee, as he asks to go off script. Let me quote the article at this point: "He speaks of trust . . . that the senator, like others in the room, shares his concerns for the emotional life of American children." He then speaks of the kind of entertainment to which children are subjected as a bombardment. He hopes we can do things differently. "From there, he describes his own lifelong effort to speak to human anxiety constructively. For Rogers, it involves puppets, music, and listening closely to children—his neighborhood expression of care. His bottom line? 'To make it clear that feelings are mentionable and manageable' and to cultivate the good feeling of self-control available to each of us whenever we are confronted by perceived conflict." The article continues:

> And then, as he nears the end of his testimony, he asks if he might recite a song whose title is the question of the hour (maybe every hour): "What do you do with the mad that you feel?" It is as if he has treated everyone present to a psychic blast of blessedness. Rogers pauses to note that the question was purloined from a child struggling with this very issue aloud. We each have the power to stop, stop, stop, Rogers instructs, as he gently strikes the table, when we have planned something, in word or action, that will go badly for ourselves and others. There is something deep within us—an inner resource, our intuition, our core—that can come to our aid when we need it most. Our feelings, we can access the realization at any moment, are mentionable and manageable. We can become what we are supposed to be.

David Dark, the author of the *America* article, writes that he and his class watched the video of this testimony and afterward generally agreed that the child's question might well be put to all who seek public office. The author himself opines that we should put the question to ourselves and then writes: "We can differ on our views of what true neighborliness consists of, but we cannot rightly leave the question of neighborliness behind. We are enjoined by the creative labor of those who precede us to find language to match our feelings and fears and to somehow do justice to what is going on. . . . We get to make more [neighborhood expressions of care] together with others, in the face of despair. One breath at a time."

When Mr. Rogers speaks of "something deep within us," I think of the Holy Spirit whom Jesus promised to send and who dwells in our hearts. All we need to do is pay attention to those deep resources given by the Spirit and to act on them. Were you reminded of anything during your prayerful reading of this section on Mr. Rogers? Perhaps you recalled your experience of listening to his shows. You may want to talk with God about your reactions and your own hopes for your life and for our country.

Your Church Community

You might reflect on your church community. Do you know and care for many of the people you pray with on Sundays? Do you take part in any of the activities of the church? Would this be a place in which you might begin to widen your circle of concern? You could talk with Jesus about your answers to these questions and see whether he has any hopes for you in this regard.

Many church communities have groups that reach out to people in need within the church community and even in the wider community. Joining one of these groups could widen your circle of concern in two ways, first by putting you in closer contact with the other group members, and second by going out to help people in need. Churches also ask for volunteers to visit the sick in hospitals and at home, to help with ministry with the dying and the bereaved, to visit prisons. These are ways of widening our circle of concern considerably. They are also ways of caring for Jesus in line with Matthew 25: "I was hungry and you fed me, naked and you clothed me, sick and you visited me," and so on.

Here's an example of such an outreach group. Joyce Hollyday spent fifteen years working as an associate editor for

Sojourners magazine in Washington, D.C. She wrote about this program in *Then Shall Your Light Rise*. I found it in *Give Us This Day: Daily Prayer for Today's Catholic*, March 2017. On Saturday mornings, she helped distribute food to poor families and individuals at Sojourners Neighbor Center. She writes:

> Every Saturday up to three hundred families came through the food line for a bag of groceries. Before opening the line, those of us serving the food clasped hands and bowed our heads. Mary Glover, an older neighborhood resident who had lived there for decades, offered a prayer. It was the same prayer every week, but it never seemed redundant. I will carry it with me forever.
>
> "We thank you, Lord, for our lying down last night and our rising up this morning. We thank you that the walls of our room were not the walls of our grave, that our bed was not our cooling board nor our bedclothes our winding-sheet. We thank you for the feet that are coming through this line for food today and the hands that are giving it out. We know, Lord, that you're coming through this line today, so help us to treat you right. Yes, Lord, help us to treat you right." (51)

This group widened its circle of concern every Saturday, and Mary Glover's prayer, every Saturday, helped them keep their minds and hearts in the right place, grateful for what they had been given and ready to meet Jesus in those they served in the food line. This example may give you food for thought or prayer.

What were your reactions to Mary Glover's prayer? Did you think of any activities you engage in where such a prayer might be appropriate? Perhaps you want to talk with Jesus about your reactions and dreams.

Welcoming the Stranger

You might ask yourself how your parish or church welcomes strangers in your midst. Often people who come to a church service for the first time feel quite alone and timid. Does your congregation try to put such people at ease? I've heard of parishes where, either at the beginning of the service or at the end, someone asks whether there are any here for the first time. They are then welcomed by an invitation to have coffee after the service or in some other way. Here is a chance to widen your circle of concern in a relatively easy way and thus make your church more welcoming and friendly.

In recent years, we have become aware of the presence among us of people whose sexual orientation may make them feel estranged from parishes and congregations: lesbians, gays, bisexuals, and those who identify themselves as transgender. For a long time, these people kept a very low profile, aware that their orientation was not acceptable. Things have changed in many parts of the world, and these people are looking for and even demanding acceptance for who they are. How welcoming is your parish to people whose sexual orientation differs from the mainstream?

In prayer you might want to talk with Jesus about how welcoming you and your parish or congregation are of gays, lesbians, and transgender people. Do you know any such people well enough to talk with them about their hopes and dreams for acceptance? Here is another issue you might want to talk over with God.

You and your parish community might also be helped by reading James Martin's latest book, *Building a Bridge: How the Catholic and the LGBT Community Can Enter into a Relationship of Respect, Compassion, and Sensitivity*, a very sensitive, caring, and theologically sound look at this topic. Martin rightly notes that building a bridge requires mutuality; both parties must treat one another with respect, compassion, and sensitivity. One of his recommendations will resonate with readers of this book: that we need to get to know people who are different from us.

An Inventory of Your Circle of Concern

It might be helpful for you to take an inventory of your circle of concern. Here's a way to do it in prayer. Remember what was said at the beginning of the book about how to start each period of prayer.

Now imagine Jesus sitting with you, and ask him to help you reflect on your circle of concern; you would be asking Jesus to show you his view of the people for whom you have genuine concern. Then, with his help, imagine a typical weekday of your life and then a weekend. What do you notice about the circle of people you meet? Whom do you look forward to seeing? Whom do you not look forward to seeing? What's the difference? Does Jesus seem interested in the difference and happy with it? Are you happy with your circle of concern? How does your circle of concern square with Jesus' parable of the sheep and the goats in Matthew 25:31–46?

All of us spend time each day outside our own small circle, for instance at work, in a gym for a workout, at a neighborhood park with our young children. You might reflect prayerfully with Jesus about the people you meet regularly. You'll probably notice that there are some people you look forward to seeing.

You can talk with Jesus about these folk, telling him what you appreciate about them. But there are also people whom you don't look forward to seeing; something about them turns you off. Why not spend some time talking with Jesus about them? You may realize that Jesus also loves and cares for them. What if you made it a habit every day before leaving home to ask Jesus to help you meet one or two of these people with openness and affection rather than suspicion and fear? I've been doing this for some years now, and it has made a big difference in my interactions with people I would ordinarily avoid. I have also noticed that some of the people now seem to be more at ease with me.

A few years ago, I had the pleasant experience of riding a few times in a car driven by a young and friendly lawyer. He greeted everyone he met and took pains to engage them in a short exchange. For example, as he went through a toll booth, he had a few friendly words with the toll collector; when he stopped at a desk in an office building to pick up something, he always spoke with the person behind the desk, often addressing the person by name. In the hallways, he greeted everyone we passed, by name if he knew it. I was very impressed, but I also noticed that the people he met were smiling as we passed. This man was making a difference in his wider world. This story reminds me that I once read of a toll station on a busy British highway. More cars went through one particular booth than any other, even though this slowed them down a bit. It turned out that the toll taker at that booth always greeted every car with a smile and a wish for a good day.

Even in our go-go world a kind word and a smile go a long way. In such small ways we can be part of God's dream of a world in which all of us live in harmony with one another. A recent homilist exhorted us to think of being "God's sunshine" for those we meet every day. It's a lovely image, isn't it? Maybe it's another way of saying what it means to live as a person made in God's image in our world. My young lawyer friend was a bit of God's sunshine to everyone he met each day, and I have no doubt that it was not an act put on for my benefit. He was the genuine article.

How did you react to this story? Have you ever met anyone like my lawyer friend? Perhaps you could spend some time talking with Jesus about your reactions and your hopes—and his.

More Widening

In the inventory of your circle of concern, you may find that there are some people you don't want to mention to Jesus because you don't want to have a different attitude toward them. In the United States, as I write, the polarization seems to revolve around attitudes toward President Trump. How do you feel about those who voted differently from you and who now seem to be listening to and reading different news media than what you watch and listen to? Because you know that Jesus asks us to love our enemies and do good to those who hate us, it might cause some bouts of conscience to realize that you have strong feelings of dislike toward those with different political leanings than yours. What can you do?

Remember that earlier we looked at the possibility (and likelihood) of not wanting to forgive someone. At that time, I suggested that we try asking God to help us *want* to forgive. You can do the same thing here.

Ask God to give you at least the desire to care for people you now don't even want to care for. You might be surprised by the results. And if there is a change in your attitude, you may be moving toward becoming part of the solution to the polarization in our country at this time.

A reminder: Take a break if you have been reading and praying for some time. If you do break, remember the suggestions for beginning any period of reading or prayer.

PRAYER SESSION #32

Going beyond Our Comfort Zone

In this session I invite you to consider and pray about some
of the more painful and difficult social issues of our time.
As you begin, remember the suggestions for any period of
prayer.

African Americans

If your skin color is white, you may not have much contact
with people of color, especially with African Americans.
African Americans have been in the United States almost
from its beginning, but they did not come here, as most of
our parents and grandparents did, on their own. They were
brought here as slaves on slave ships. That history of slavery
almost destroyed the country at the time of the Civil War
and has left our so-called melting pot with an almost perma-
nent underclass of American citizens who are only with great

difficulty accepted into the mainstream, no matter how well they succeed in education and in income. Periodically in our history, it seemed as though the racial divide was finally being bridged, but racial prejudice continues to bedevil us as a people to this day.

For example, if you are white, did any African Americans turn up in the inventory of your circle of concern? I wonder how many of us whites have spent time in prayer talking with Jesus about our own attitudes toward and relationships with people of color. Let's give it a try in this section of the book, for our own sake as Christians and for the sake of our country, which still experiences racial divides and tensions that are ominous for our future.

If we do find that our circle of concern does not include African Americans, what can we do? It will not surprise you that I start with the suggestion of a prayerful reflection. You could spend some quiet time with Jesus, talking about your own feelings about the racial tensions in our country. Be honest with him about your own reactions and feelings.

For example, you may feel kind of helpless and even hopeless about the racial situation we face in the United States. You may feel that you are not prejudiced and be angry that this topic has even been raised in this book. You may feel that African Americans are being given privileges these days that your own parents and, perhaps, you yourself did not have, that you and your parents had to work hard to get where you are now. Whatever you feel, be honest with Jesus, and take time to listen to what he might want to say or to suggest to you.

Once this conversation has begun, you may find some of your feelings and attitudes changing. Remember that the conversation started because you realized that your circle of concern includes few, if any, African Americans at a time when race relations in our country seem constantly in the news. Just by engaging in this kind of conversation with Jesus you are opening the possibility of becoming part of the solution rather than part of the problem.

The "Talk"

Most of us white Americans know little of the experience of growing up as an African American. Another way to move ourselves toward becoming part of the solution to the racial tension in our country might be to learn something about the experiences of African Americans. If you are lucky enough to have become friendly with people of color, you might ask them if their parents ever gave "the talk" to their sons as they entered their teen years. This "talk," you will find, is not about the birds and the bees but about how the boy should behave if ever he is stopped by the police. African American parents are terrified that their young sons will be hurt or shot by the police; they have seen or heard of it happening too often not to take this threat seriously. They teach their sons to be properly subservient and polite even if they have done nothing wrong.

Michael Eric Dyson, an African American preacher and professor who was born poor in Detroit, recently published the book *Tears We Cannot Stop*. In it he tells the following story: When he was seventeen, he was driving his father's car with his brother and a friend as passengers. The car had been stolen earlier but found by the police and returned to the family. However, the police had failed to remove the car from the list of stolen cars, and the Dysons were not informed of this. The boys were stopped by an unmarked police car with four policemen in it. They were frisked, but two of the police had drawn their guns. Dyson wanted to show them proof that the car belonged to his father and started to speak to the officer:

> "Sir, I'm reaching into my back pocket to get my wallet that has the car's registration". . . . Before I could fetch it the cop brought the butt of his gun sharply across my back and knocked me to the ground.
>
> "Nigger, if you move again without me telling you to I'll put a bullet through your fucking head."

I rose to my feet. Slowly. Deliberately. Showing complete deference. Barely breathing. Barely raising my head above a supplicating bow.

The cop gave him permission to get the wallet and the registration papers. The police found out that the car did belong to their father. Dyson writes: "They offered no apology, and without a single word, with just a nod, they sent us on our way (171–72)."

How do you react to this story? Talk with Jesus about your reactions, no matter what they were. Don't try to be politically correct with Jesus. It won't work. You'll both know that you're not telling the whole truth. You may not like some of your reactions, but that's no reason not to be honest with Jesus or indeed with any good friend. And if it did not occur to you to do so, talk to Jesus about your reactions to what the cop said and did. He, too, is a child of God and made in God's image. It's possible that he and his fellow officers were at least a bit scared as they approached that car. Much of our anger and bluster grows out of fear. It does not excuse such behavior, but it might help us recognize ourselves in them too. I don't believe Jesus wants us to trade one kind of prejudice for another. Do you?

It might help you walk around in the shoes of an African American to read the whole of Dyson's book, which is subtitled *A Sermon to White America*. Dyson writes the book to convince white Americans to recognize how our white privilege goes unacknowledged by us and allows us to tolerate what it does to African Americans. Another recent best seller might also help: Ta-Nehisi Coates's letter to his son, *Between the World and Me*. Both books tell the truth unflinchingly and with strong language, but they can go a long way toward widening our circle of concern.

Of course, nothing can take the place of developing real friendships with people of color, people outside our race or neighborhood or subculture. Maybe prayer and reading will open our hearts and minds to becoming more open to such a widening of our circle of concern.

"I Was in Prison and You Visited Me"

Earlier I mentioned Darrell Jones, the man who was just freed after thirty-two years in prison for a murder he did not commit. I first got to know him through letters. In his third or fourth letter he asked if I knew that he was African American. Tears came to my eyes as I read this. To think that he would be afraid that I would not continue to write to him because of his race! That brought home to me the kind of prejudice African Americans experience. In time I began to visit Darrell, and we have become close. As a result, I have come into close contact with an African American and have met and love some of Darrell's family and friends, and I have also come to some knowledge of the prison system and of prisoners. In Matthew 25 Jesus says, "I was in prison and you did not visit me" as one of the reasons for condemnation. It turns out that African Americans and Hispanic Americans are much more likely to be imprisoned than whites. A visit to a prison might widen your circle on two fronts.

Did you know that in the past thirty to forty years the prison population of the United States has increased enormously so that now about 2.3 million people are incarcerated in federal, state, local, and military prisons as well as in juvenile correctional facilities and detention centers, among other forms of incarceration? At the same time, about 820,000 people are on parole and close to 3.8 million are on probation. The United States has one of the largest prison populations in the entire world. Compared to their percentages within the overall population, racial and ethnic minority groups are overrepresented in our prison: approximately 71 percent of all male and female inmates in United States correctional facilities are black and Hispanic.

Reading may widen your circle of concern to take in the justice system in the United States. I have found the following books eye-opening: Michelle Alexander's *The New Jim*

Crow: Mass Incarceration in the Age of Colorblindness, Revised Edition, and Elizabeth Hinton's *From the War on Poverty to the War on Crime: The Making of Mass Incarceration in America.*

Alexander shows how the War on Drugs led to mass incarceration in the United States, the greatest burden being borne by people of color from the poorer sections of our country's cities. Alexander believes that the dream of a country that is colorblind is a danger. Racial differences will always be with us. The real danger, she believes, is that we "will choose to be blind to injustice and the suffering of others. . . . Seeing race is not the problem. Refusing to care for the people we see is the problem. . . . We should hope not for a colorblind society but instead for a world in which we can see each other fully, learn from each other, and do what we can to respond to each other with love" (243-44). Alexander believes that changes in our laws, while needed, are not what is most needed. If our hearts are not changed, if we do not begin to care about what is happening to people of color in our inner cities as a result of the wars on poverty, on drugs, and on crime, these poor people will suffer what white America would not tolerate if it were inflicted on their neighborhoods, where often the same rate of illegal drug usage goes on with relative impunity.

(By the way, why do we declare war against drugs, crime, or poverty? What does a war ever do but lead to another war?)

> You might want to talk with Jesus about your reactions to what you have just read and see how the conversation develops.

Once again it comes down to the questions "Who is my neighbor?" and "For whom do I really care?" If you want to get a sense of how racial prejudice leads to shocking injustice and cruelty in the United States justice system, you might read Bryan Stevenson's *Just Mercy: A Story of Justice and Redemption*. Stevenson's book will break your heart but also uplift you. The Jesuit Gregory Boyle has written a heartbreaking yet hopeful book about his work with Hispanic gang members in the Jesuit parish in Los Angeles, *Tattoos on the Heart: The Power of Boundless Compassion*. It's an extraordinary example of how "boundless compassion" does change the lives of people who seem caught in a hopeless situation.

> Perhaps you can talk to Jesus about how you might grow in care for the plight of prisoners in the United States.

Immigrants and Refugees

One of the great crises of our world as I write this book has to do with the tremendous increase in the number of people who are leaving their homelands to seek some safe place to live and work. Pope Francis has made this crisis one of his major concerns almost from the beginning of his pontificate. All of us have been touched by the plight of refugees fleeing from famine and war, taking great risks to bring themselves and their families to safety. What to do about the floods of requests for asylum and safety has caused major conflicts in the United States and in Europe.

Most of us can do little to change the circumstances that have led to the present crisis. But we can do something about our attitudes toward immigrants and refugees who come to our own country.

You might want to spend some time with Jesus talking about your own attitudes toward the crisis and toward immigrants. Again, with Jesus, honesty is the best policy. Forget about political correctness when you talk with him. Just let him know what your real feelings and attitudes are, and see how he reacts to you. Remember that he and his family were refugees in Egypt for a while to escape the threats of Herod the Great and that he lived under the occupation of the Roman conquerors all his life. You could ask him how he felt in Egypt and toward the Romans later in life. It could be a very interesting and insightful conversation. These kinds of conversations can lead to our becoming better images of God as we take on more of the attitudes of Jesus.

In recent years, many of the immigrants and refugees who have come to the United States are Muslims. Ask yourself about your attitude toward Muslims. Do you know any Muslims? Many Christians, it seems, fear and mistrust Muslims. In "A Conversation on Why Catholics Need to Dialogue with Muslims," posted on the *America* Web site for February 2, 2018, Zac Davis cites a study done by the Center for Applied Research in the Apostolate at Georgetown University. In that study, one in three Roman Catholics admits to having unfavorable views about Muslims. Moreover, this was true for Catholics of all ages and ethnicities.

You might want to talk to Jesus about your own attitudes, recalling that in Matthew 25, Jesus distinguishes the sheep from the goats by whether they welcomed him when he was a stranger. It might be an interesting and helpful conversation.

Joining God in Caring for Our Planet

Early in this book, we reflected prayerfully on the biblical story of creation in which human beings are created in God's image and likeness and asked by God to cooperate with God in caring for the rest of creation. The kingdom of God, I noted, could be defined as a world in which human beings live in friendship and harmony with God, with one another, and with the whole of the creation. Gradually, over the past century, we have come to realize that our planet is in need of our care, and the concern has become more and more widespread. In his encyclical *Laudato Si'*, Pope Francis makes an impassioned plea to all of us to take the danger to our planetary home very seriously. Here is another area in which we are asked to widen our circle of concern.

Why not begin by returning to chapter 1 of Genesis, this time asking God to help you recognize how precious everything God creates is to God. Take time to let that sink in. Talk to God about your own feelings, reactions, and thoughts. Then you might focus on God's request that we humans cooperate with God in taking care of creation.

You might want to read and discuss with a group the encyclical itself. As with many of Pope Francis's writings, this one is relatively devoid of jargon and rather straightforward. It lends itself to a prayerful reading. You won't be surprised that I suggest having a talk with Jesus about your own use of planetary resources such as water, energy, food, and transportation. You might follow up the conversation with other conversations with those close to you: your family, fellow workers, friends. At the least, such conversations might move you toward becoming part of the solution, not just part of the problem. Who knows what will come of such small beginnings?

Doing Our Part

By engaging in these kinds of conversations with Jesus and with those around us, I believe, we take seriously God's desire that we cooperate with God's great dream of bringing about what Jesus called the kingdom of God. On our planet, at least, God wants a world where we live in harmony with

God, with one another, and with the whole of creation. God invites each of us to do our part in our small and big ways to make the world a more harmonious and life-giving place for all. We can't do everything; we are not God. But we are created in God's image, and we can choose to live out that identity. God dreams of us living out his image and character wherever we are—at home, in our neighborhoods, in our churches, in our jobs, in our play, in the voting booth, in our contacts with our elected representatives, in all we do. That's our part to play in God's great work.

It's our glory and, alas, also our shame that we are called to be images of God—our shame because we so often fail. But God has never given up on us, and never will, thank God. So let's keep asking God's help every day to live as the people God created us to be.

"You Don't Do God Alone"

This was the title of a short article by Bill McGarvey in *America* (October 24, 2016). McGarvey is right. Believers have always found that they need to belong to some kind of community. You might say that we wither and die without others. Persons are not built to live in silos; we need others. It surely means something profound that God's very self is relational, mysteriously Three who are One God. And we are made in God's image and likeness. We need one another to become our best selves, to become the images of God we are created to be. McGarvey cites the experience of the founders of Alcoholics Anonymous and all those countless people who have followed them in finding sobriety and sanity through their fellowship, their community. He cites Bill W., one of the founders: "We must find some spiritual basis for living, else we die." He follows up with a citation from his cofounder, Dr. Bob: "The spiritual approach was as useless as any other if you soaked it up like a sponge and kept it to yourself." In other words, any spirituality worth its salt must be shared. A me-and-Jesus-alone spirituality is a lost cause.

So, while I have, without embarrassment, made many suggestions in this book to engage in conversations with Jesus, I hope that I have also gotten across the need to share this journey of becoming a lover of God and neighbor with others. We need one another. In fact, don't we find that our caring for others is not just for others' sakes but also for ourselves? I have mentioned more than once that caring for others is the best way for us to be deeply happy people. People who let us love them and care for them are doing us a great favor, aren't they? Indeed, we can't do God alone.

Purring for God

As a final prayerful reflection on the first great commandment, let's recall Luke's account of Jesus curing the ten lepers.

> On the way to Jerusalem Jesus was going through the region between Samaria and Galilee. As he entered a village, ten lepers approached him. Keeping their distance, they called out, saying, "Jesus, Master, have mercy on us!" When he saw them, he said to them, "Go and show yourselves to the priests." And as they went, they were made clean. Then one of them, when he saw that he was healed, turned back, praising God with a loud voice. He prostrated himself at Jesus' feet and thanked him. And he was a Samaritan. Then Jesus asked, "Were not ten made clean? But the other nine, where are they? Was none of them found to return and give praise to God except this foreigner?" Then he said to him, "Get up and go on your way; your faith has made you well." (Luke 17:11–19)

What difference did it make for the Samaritan to come back and give thanks? All ten were cured and were joyful and perhaps grateful. Jesus didn't take back the cures of the other nine because they didn't give thanks, did he?

Try to imagine the Samaritan meeting the other nine after he had thanked Jesus. Would he not have said something like this? "You should have seen the gleam of joy in his eyes when he saw me at his feet. He spoke with me, and I with him. It was a touch of heaven, I thought. You should have come with me. It was really wonderful. He was overjoyed that I was healed and that I came back to thank him. I felt that he appreciated my consideration of his feelings." How do you react to that scenario?

One thing we should never forget as we pray to love God with our whole minds, hearts, and souls is that we are being drawn into a *mutual* relationship. God reacts to us, and we react to God; it's a friendship that develops between us.

Reflection on this passage reminded me of a poem by Edward Hirsch and some experiences of my own with a cat. Hirsch's poem is called "Wild Gratitude" and details his own experience of petting his cat, Zooey, as well as the experience of the British poet Christopher Smart with his cat, Jeoffry, both of whom "can teach us how to praise—purring / In their own language, / Wreathing themselves in the living fire." One of my friends has a male Maine coon cat named Chi who has come to trust me. On occasion he shows that he wants me to pet him by turning over on his back so that I can scratch his belly. He purrs and writhes with what I take for joy and what feels like "wild gratitude" to me. I enjoy it as much as he seems to. I am happy to make him happy and delighted that he enjoys my company.

These two cat stories lead me to wonder if God enjoys our love as much as we enjoy loving God and being loved by God. I leave our reflections on the first great commandment with this thought. Perhaps when we let God love us, we love God. If so, let's purr for God with gratitude.

A God's-Eye View of the World

Recently I reread Frederick Buechner's four novels about the loveable and broken preacher Leo Bebb, *Lion Country*, *Open Heart*, *Love Feast*, and *Treasure Hunt*. The four together are called *The Book of Bebb*. They are funny, endearing, outrageous, and utterly captivating. When I finished this second reading, I realized that I had come to care for all of the many characters that people these stories, including the "evil brother" of the last novel. Fairly soon after I finished rereading Buechner's novels, I read Ann Patchett's latest novel

Commonwealth and had a similar realization. As was true when I read her earlier novels, I had come to care for all the many characters in this one, even the ones who at first turned me off.

It occurred to me that these novelists had something of a God's-eye view of human beings to be able to imagine so many broken and bent people who are, with all their faults, foibles, and sins, still loveable. I also realized that I am most attracted to novelists such as these two. That may say something rather weird about me; who knows? But when I read novels nowadays, I tend to quit reading when I notice that I don't really care for any of the characters. I feel that the novelist doesn't care for them either. (This is a change for me. I used to finish anything I had begun to read, no matter what I felt. I've grown wiser or less tolerant, or maybe I realize that I don't have forever on my hands in this life.)

This rumination on novels leads me to this prayerful reflection on love of neighbor. What I take to be the worldview of Frederick Buechner and Ann Patchett is one I have been daily praying to have for some years now: to be able to approach everyone I meet today with openness and affection rather than suspicion and fear. That desire is what we have been praying and reflecting about in these last sessions on the great commandment, love of neighbor. If all of us were to pray for this blessing in our interior lives daily, imagine what our world would look like. It would be a place where God's kingdom had come on heaven and on earth, as we are urged to pray in the Our Father. We would surely be more like the images of God we are created to be, and our world would be a far, far better place for all of us. Maybe this paragraph will give you something to talk over with God.

In *Persons in Relation*, the Scottish philosopher John Macmurray describes the ideal toward which our creation as persons moves us, namely toward "a universal community of persons in which each cares for all the others and no one [cares] for himself" (159). Macmurray succinctly describes a community of all human beings in which no one has to care for him/herself because no one has anything to fear; we would all know that everyone else cares for us and is looking for our good. This would indeed be the kingdom of God, wouldn't it?

In fact, God is this ideal "community," Three so mysteriously in love with one another that they are One God. And God has created us to be like God and to join God in helping to bring about this kind of community. It's not a chimera, a pipe dream; it's God's dream for us and what God has made a reality in the life, death, and resurrection of Jesus. Loving

God and neighbor really can change the world. In fact, God is counting on us. Let's keep praying that we might become more and more like God in our dealings with all those we meet each day. We have nothing to lose but the chains of our fears. Maybe you can hear God "purring" with love as you end this journey. I hope so.

On Discernment

How Can I Know It's God Communicating? Some Simple Rules of Thumb for Discernment

In the *Spiritual Exercises*, Ignatius has an appendix called "Rules for the Discernment of Spirits." He says that they are "rules by which to perceive and understand to some extent the various movements produced in the soul: the good that they may be accepted, and the bad, that they may be rejected" (313). In this appendix I want to present some rules of thumb based on what Ignatius says that may assist you to make sense of some of the interior movements of your mind, heart, and body that occur when you engage in dialogue with the Lord.

Let me say immediately that these rules of thumb are of a rather general kind; at times you will need the help of a spiritual director or of some other person you trust to help you to sort out what is really happening in your heart. There is always the danger of self-delusion in the matter of developing one's relationship with God. However, I also believe that some spiritual masters have made the discernment of spirits seem more esoteric and difficult than is the case. Ignatius himself began to discern the spirits when he was a spiritual infant and theologically illiterate.

The best way to start, therefore, might be to tell the story of Ignatius's first discernment of spirits, which he describes in his "Reminiscences." Growing up, he was, by his own admission, something of a hell-raiser. Though destined for the clerical state by his father (he had received the tonsure), he spent his youth and young adulthood pursuing a career as a courtier and warrior. He was also a womanizer. In the battle of Pamplona his legs were badly wounded by a cannonball. Brought back to the castle of Loyola, he suffered great pains in order to have his bad leg straightened so that he could still cut a fine figure as a soldier and courtier. During his convalescence, the only books available were a life of Christ and a book of the lives of saints. This reading caused him to begin to daydream about following Christ as had St. Francis of Assisi and St. Dominic. He dreamt of living and dying in the Holy Land working for Christ. These daydreams alternated with other daydreams in which Ignatius did great deeds of valor as a knight and warrior to win the favor of a great lady. He enjoyed both sets of daydreams and for a long time did not notice that they had different emotional effects after he finished them. When he finished the dreams of doing great deeds as a warrior, he says, "he would find himself dry and discontented." But when he finished the dreams of doing great things for Christ, "he would remain content and happy." Then he goes on to say that,

> he wasn't investigating this, nor stopping to ponder this difference, until one time his eyes were opened a little, and he began to marvel at this difference in kind and to reflect on it, picking up from experience that from some thoughts he would be left sad and from others happy, and little by little coming to know the difference in kind of spirits that were stirring; the one from the devil, and the other from God (15).

This story should take some of the mystery out of the process of discernment of spirits. First of all, the interior movements Ignatius speaks of are the ordinary ones we experience all the time, happiness and joy versus sadness and dryness. Second, Ignatius finally paid attention to the difference in his emotional life caused by these sets of daydreams. Third, Ignatius came to the conclusion that these different emotional states resulted from thoughts and dreams caused on the one hand by God and on the other by the devil. In his rules for discernment of spirits, he does not attribute all interior movements contrary to God's intentions to the devil; they can also come from our own resistance to the call of God. The main point to get from this story is that paying attention to the different emotional states caused in us by thoughts, dreams, contemplations, and actions can help us to decide what God is communicating to us and what is not from God. That is what discernment of spirits is all about.

The first rule of thumb I suggest is that you look at your ordinary orientation with regard to God and to your life as a Christian. Do you try to lead a good Christian life insofar as possible? Or are you someone who cuts corners with regard to your Christian life? As an example of the latter, think of a landlord who gouges his tenants and provides few services to make their living even halfway decent. Suppose that he were to try to engage in a session of prayer. What do you think would happen? Probably he would begin to feel the pangs of conscience as he realized how good God has been to him. He might also feel some relief from these pangs of conscience when he had thoughts like these: "These tenants are a lazy lot anyway; at least I'm giving them a roof over their heads." Ignatius would say that the pangs of conscience come from God and that the rationalizations that give relief come from the evil spirit or from his own unwillingness to change his lifestyle.

What about the person who is trying to live a decent Christian life even if not perfectly, say, a working mother and wife who tries her best to do an honest day's work and to take care of her family obligations? When she begins to pray, she might feel great joy and peace and look forward to prayer. Then she might experience some anxieties, feeling that she was being too proud to expect God to speak to her or that taking time for prayer like this was a luxury she could ill afford. I remember a woman who had three very moving and wonderful days of prayer on retreat who suddenly had the thought, "This is too highfalutin for the likes of me." As a result, her prayer became dry and boring until she realized that fear of too much closeness to God had produced the disturbing thought. Ignatius would say that in a case like this, the positive experiences came from God or the good spirit who wants to make everything easy for her and the troubling thoughts came from the bad spirit or from her fears of closeness to God.

So, the first rule of thumb urges you to establish the general orientation of your life. If you are not in tune with God in your life, you can expect that God will try to get you to change your life; you will feel pangs of conscience about aspects of your life. These pangs of conscience, however, will not lead to anxious, scrupulous examinations of all your motivations; they will gently point out where you have gone wrong. The bad spirit, or your own desire not to change your life, will try to whisper blandishments in your ear to convince you all is OK. On the other hand, if you are trying to live in tune with God's intention, God will console you, help you to move forward, encourage you in your efforts to live a good life. But the bad spirit, or your own fear of change, will try to make you leery of developing a closer relationship with God. For example, Ignatius had the thought at one point during his time at Manresa, *And how will you be able to put up with this (namely his ascetical life and prayers) for the seventy years ahead of you?* Ignatius quite rightly answered that no one could guarantee that he would live for even one more day. The great temptation of an alcoholic is to imagine the many years of sobriety he or she will have to endure; hence the advice of the A.A. program to take one day at a time.

The second rule of thumb follows from the first. God wants us to be happy and fulfilled. But the only way we can be happy and fulfilled is to be in tune with God's desire for the world and for us. For those who try to live a good life in tune with God's intention, consolation is the order of the day for the most part. This does not mean that life will be without pain and suffering; it means that God wants to be a consoling presence to us even in the inevitable pains and sufferings life has in store. If this is true, then the terrible mental agony and torture scrupulous people go through is not from God. After all, scrupulous people are trying to live in tune with God. Ignatius himself, during his early days at Manresa, was plagued by scruples, fearing that he had not confessed all his sins. Things got so bad that he contemplated suicide. But at this point in his life he was trying with great fervor, indeed with excessive fervor, to live his life in accordance with God's intention. He finally came to the conclusion that these scrupulous thoughts could not be from God.

As a result of these two rules of thumb, we can define spiritual consolation and spiritual desolation along Ignatian lines. Spiritual consolation is, obviously, something positive that is experienced. The word *spiritual* does not mean that the consolation goes on in us without our awareness. Spiritual consolation refers to any experience of desire for God, of distaste for one's past sins, of sympathy for Jesus or for any other suffering person. It refers, in other words, to "every increase of hope, faith, and charity, to all interior happiness which calls and attracts to heavenly things and to the salvation of one's soul, leaving the soul quiet and at peace in her Creator and Lord" (*Sp. Ex.* 316). The epistle to the Galatians lists the fruit of the Spirit as "love, joy, peace, patience, kindness, generosity, faithfulness, gentleness, and self-control" (Galatians 5:22–23). When you experience this group of movements in your being, you can be relatively sure that you are being moved by God.

Spiritual desolation is the contrary of spiritual consolation. Ignatius gives these examples:

> darkness and disturbance in the soul, attraction towards what is low and of the earth, anxiety arising from various agitations and temptations. All this tends to a lack of confidence in which the soul is without hope and without love; one finds oneself thoroughly lazy, lukewarm, sad, and as though cut off from one's Creator and Lord (*Sp. Ex.* 317).

Provided we are trying to live a good life, the experiences of feeling out of sorts, ill at ease, anxious, unhappy, listless, etc., are experiences of spiritual desolation. They do not come from God.

These definitions lead us to our third rule of thumb. When we are experiencing spiritual desolation, it is not a good time to make any major decisions about our life's course. Rather, we should beg God for patience and for some light as to the causes of the desolation. We might look back to the last time when we experienced consolation and then try to examine what might have led to the desolation. Sometimes we will discover that the desolation appeared when we became afraid of some new step forward in our relationship with God or of some change of direction in our life that seemed to be demanded if we were to remain true to ourselves and to God. For example, I might notice that desolation began when I saw Jesus forgive Peter and thought, with repugnance, about forgiving someone who had injured me. After that I avoided thinking about Jesus and Peter. But we also need to remind ourselves that we often cannot figure out the source of our desolation; no one experiences a steady diet of consolation; then we beg God for help to endure the desolation until consolation returns, as it will.

The fourth rule of thumb has to do with times of consolation. In such times remember to be grateful to God for this gift. It is undeserved. You are happy because God has been good enough to draw you to a deeper union and to living out God's intention for you.

The fifth and final rule of thumb is to be open and honest with your spiritual director or with someone else you trust about what is actually going on in you when you try to pray. Such openness will keep you from remaining long in desolation or false consolation. By false consolation I mean a kind of euphoria that does not conform to what is actually going on in your life. An example: a person who feels no sadness at all at the loss of a loved one but only joy that the loved one is "in heaven." Another: a married man in his late forties who finds "new life" and "great peace" in a fundamentalist church group that estranges him from his wife, his family, and his friends. Another: a religious brother who becomes greatly enthused about becoming a missionary in Brazil but has no talent for learning languages and, in fact, is greatly needed in his present work. (This chapter is a slight adaptation of an appendix published in my *What Do I Want in Prayer?* Mahwah, NJ: Paulist Press, 1994. I thank the editor of Paulist Press for permission to reprint.)

Acknowledgments

Just as one cannot do God alone, one cannot write a book alone. Of course, the writer is alone at his/her desk or computer, but he/she also depends on so many others for nurture and encouragement. I want to say thanks to the many who have been with me as I wrote this book and brought it to publication. Let me start with the one who makes all things possible, God, Father, Son, and Holy Spirit, for being with me at every step and especially at those times when I seemed stuck and did not know how to move forward. Thanks be to God, always.

I have been a Jesuit for sixty-eight years; I am full of gratitude for my Jesuit brothers who have supported me for all these years, and especially to my brothers at Campion Center, my community for twenty years and counting. Thanks to Robert J. Levens, SJ, who finished serving as our superior on June 1, 2017, having been our very caring and supportive leader for seven years. I am grateful to my sisters, Peggy, Mary, and Kathleen, who have cheered me on all these years. Once again I express my gratitude to Marika Geoghegan for her friendship and encouragement at every step of the way toward the finish of this book. I also want to thank all those who have trusted me as their spiritual director over many years. They have taught me so much by their own love of God and openness in speaking of their experiences of God. What a gift!

Once I finished the draft of the book, I needed feedback, and I received it from the following friends who read the manuscript with loving care: Joseph A. Appleyard, SJ, Carol Johannes, OP, James J. Martin, SJ, William C. Russell, SJ, Simon E. Smith, SJ, and Judy Talvacchia. Their suggestions and corrections made this a much better book. What great friends! I want to single out Si Smith, SJ, who went over the manuscript with a fine-tooth comb and helped to clean up any number of mistakes and omissions.

Joe Durepos of Loyola Press has been a very supportive friend for many years. He came to visit me at a critical time when I was faltering in my confidence that I could finish the book; his words of encouragement proved all the difference.

After that visit I was able, by the grace of God and that support, to finish the draft within a short time. Thanks, Joe.

Vinita Wright, my editor at Loyola Press, really understood my hope that this book would be an invitation to prayer. She suggested cutting the manuscript into smaller, more reader-friendly sections, and then went at the process of cutting with her usual attention to detail and great writing skill. The book in its final form owes everything to her skill and great writer's touch. A big thank you to Vinita and also to Susan Taylor, who did a superb and meticulous piece of copy editing, for which I am very grateful.

I have twice used ideas from this book for guided retreats at Campion Renewal Center with groups of thirty to forty people, who gave me very positive feedback. I was asked to give a Lenten series of talks using the manuscript at St. Gerard Majella Parish in Canton, Massachusetts, in 2017. And in Lent of this year I gave two talks on ways to grow in love of God and neighbor at the joined parishes of St. Edward in Medfield, Massachusetts, and St. Jude in Norfolk, Massachusetts.

Finally, I am grateful to all those who have written or spoken to me about what my writing has contributed to the growth of their friendship with God. I count on their prayers and continued support as I move into the latter stages of my life. Once again, thanks be to God and thanks to all.

I have dedicated this book to two very special people in my life. Bill Russell, SJ, has been a dear friend for many years. He is willing to tell his friends the truth and has a great sense of humor as well as great love for God. Darrell Jones was imprisoned for thirty-two years for a murder he did not commit. He and I have been close friends for some ten to twelve years. On December 21, 2017, he finally was freed after a judge overturned his conviction. Free at last, he continues to amaze with his goodness and desire to help others. I am proud that he calls me "Dad." Both of these men show their love of God by their love of neighbor.

Selected Bibliography

Alexander, Michelle. *The New Jim Crow: Mass Incarceration in the Age of Colorblindness,* Revised Edition. New York: Free Press, 2012.

Alighieri, Dante. *The Divine Comedy,* trans. John Ciardi. New York: New American Library, 2003.

Augustine. *Confessions,* translated and with an introduction by R. S. Pine-Coffin. Harmondsworth, Middlesex, England: Penguin, 1961.

Buechner, Frederick. *The Sacred Journey.* New York: Harper & Row, 1982.

——*The Eyes of the Heart: A Memoir of the Lost and Found.* San Francisco: HarperCollins, 2000.

Dark, David. "In the Age of Trump, Can Mr. Rogers Help Us Manage Our Anger?" *America* (May 1, 2017): 27–33.

Davies, Oliver. *A Theology of Compassion: Metaphysics of Difference and the Renewal of Tradition.* Grand Rapids, MI: Eerdmans, 2001.

Dostoevsky, Fyodor. *The Brothers Karamazov,* trans. Richard Pevear and Larissa Volokhonsky. San Francisco: North Point Press, 1990.

Doyle, Brian. Cited in *Give Us This Day: Daily Prayer for Today's Catholic.* Collegeville, MN: Liturgical Press, January 2017: 290–291.

Dyson, Michael Eric. *Tears We Cannot Stop: A Sermon to White America.* New York: St. Martin's Press, 2017.

Ellsberg, Robert. *The Saints' Guide to Happiness: Everyday Wisdom from the Lives of the Saints.* New York: North Point Press, 2003.

Genovese, Nick. "My Family Disagrees about Donald Trump—But That Won't Divide Us." *America* December 7, 2016. www.americamagazine.org/politics-society/2016/12/07/my-family-disagrees-about-donald-trump-wont-divide-us.

Hollyday, Joyce. *Then Shall Your Light Rise.* Nashville: Upper Room Books, 1997.

Ignatius of Loyola. *Personal Writings,* trans. Joseph A. Munitiz and Philip Endean. London: Penguin Books, 1996.

James, P. D., *Original Sin.* New York: Time Warner, 1994.

Levertov, Denise. *The Stream and the Sapphire.* New York: New Directions, 1997.

Lohfink, Gerhard. *Is This All There is? On Resurrection and Eternal Life,* trans. Linda M. Maloney. Collegeville, MN: Liturgical Press Academic, 2018.

Macmurray, John. *Persons in Relation.* Atlantic Highlands, NJ: Humanities Press, 1991.

Martin, James. "A Week in Rome with Jesuits, and I Saw God at Work Far beyond the Vatican." *America.* January 2, 2017. www.americamagazine.org/faith/2016/12/16/ james-martin-week-rome-jesuits-and-i-saw-god-work-far-beyond-vatican.

O'Connell, James J. *Stories from the Shadows: Reflections of a Street Doctor.* Boston: BHCHP Press, 2015.

Rutledge, Fleming. *The Crucifixion: Understanding the Death of Jesus Christ.* Grand Rapids, MI: Eerdmans, 2015.

Wright, N. T. *Paul and the Faithfulness of God: Christian Origins and the Question of God.* Minneapolis, MN: Fortress, 2013.

Wright, Tom. *Matthew for Everyone.* Louisville, KY: Westminster John Knox Press, 2004.